Life's a Stage

At TEDxUoNMalaysia in February 2020 with my talk titled "Better, Not Bitter".

Life's a Stage

Stories & Lessons for An Empowered Life

FREDA LIU

Marshall Cavendish
Editions

Published by Marshall Cavendish Editions
An imprint of Marshall Cavendish International

A member of the
Times Publishing Group

Other Marshall Cavendish Offices:
Marshall Cavendish Corporation, 800 Westchester Ave, Suite N-641, Rye Brook,
NY 10573, USA • Marshall Cavendish International (Thailand) Co Ltd, 253 Asoke,
16th Floor, Sukhumvit 21 Road, Klongtoey Nua, Wattana, Bangkok 10110, Thailand •
Marshall Cavendish (Malaysia) Sdn Bhd, Times Subang, Lot 46, Subang Hi-Tech
Industrial Park, Batu Tiga, 40000 Shah Alam, Selangor Darul Ehsan, Malaysia

Marshall Cavendish is a registered trademark of Times Publishing Limited

National Library Board, Singapore Cataloguing in Publication Data

Name(s): Liu, Freda.
Title: Life's a stage : stories & lessons for an empowered life / Freda Liu.
Description: Singapore : Marshall Cavendish Editions, [2021]
Identifier(s): OCN 1225874463 | ISBN 978-981-49-2827-4 (paperback)
Subject(s): LCSH: Liu, Freda. | Celebrities--Malaysia--Biography. | Radio
    personalities--Malaysia--Biography. | Television personalities--Malaysia
    --Biography. | Orators--Malaysia--Biography.
Classification: DDC 791.44028092--dc23

Printed in Singapore

Back cover, photo on left, image credit: Grant Corban

CONTENTS

FOREWORD

Shakespeare wrote, "All the world's a stage, and all the men and women merely players. They have their exits and their entrances; And one man in his time plays many parts."

Shakespeare's words definitely hold true for Freda Liu. In the ten or so years that I have known her, Freda has played many parts. I met Freda when she was a radio interviewer. An interviewer who had the gift of making you feel comfortable from the very start. A highly polished interviewer. And, that voice! Media and Freda's voice were like a marriage made in heaven!

Since then, Freda has played many other parts, with each part leading to a bigger role in her public life. Over the years, Freda has become known, liked and in demand beyond radio. She became an author, a speaker, a person who inspired countless others. And more.

Behind the public part, there is the private life of Freda. I have seen her deal with extreme pain in her life with dignity. The public was being educated and entertained by radio Freda. Little did they know what was happening "behind the curtain" of Freda's private life. Little did the world see her working so hard to balance motherhood with the many demands on her career.

So, how do we sum up, in a few words, who Freda is? First, she's an ordinary person just like you and me. Freda has shown us that an ordinary person can achieve extraordinary things. Second, Freda is the "real deal". You will experience that same authentic Freda on stage and over coffee. I am finding myself wanting to use so many other adjectives to describe Freda. Humble. Yes, Very humble and grounded. When you speak with Freda, you will find that, despite the varied and exciting things going in her life, she is interested in you! Freda has not let her celebrity change the essence of who she is. This is Freda's sixth book, written amid a busy public and work schedule. Freda is focused. Hardworking. Intelligent.

Whoa, am I getting carried away here? Not at all. I could go on.

So, what has made Freda the person that she is? In reading her engaging stories in the pages to follow, you get some clues. And more importantly, the stories in this book will move you to reflect on your own life. How do we think? How do we believe in ourselves? How do we handle hardships? How do we grow through the experiences in our lives? That's what the book has done for me.

I know that you will enjoy reading about the many stages in Freda's life. And, I have a feeling that, as Freda's star shines more brightly, there will be a sequel to follow!

George Aveling
Group CEO & International Partner
TMI Consulting

Image credit: Grant Corban

SETTING THE STAGE

You Can Have Everything in Life ... Just Not at the Same Time

Why am I writing another book? While all my previous books have included glimpses of my life, they featured other women, people and organisations. A dear friend told me that I was still masking myself and that my story (and we all have one) could serve as a guide for others.

This may be because I have reached half a century in age, and been asked a lot of questions about life. I wanted to share the lessons I have learned over the years (and mistakes I have made) and some of the strategies I have used in understanding life stages, which are not dictated by age but circumstances at the time. When you understand life in stages and what you can do best at the moment with an eye on the future, with some planning and execution, you'll be prepared as life rolls on.

All these thoughts and ideas have been brought together by a lifetime of reading, listening to audio materials and attending seminars. It has helped tremendously that my work in a business radio station involves speaking to experts around the world from fields including business, technology and personal development. What has also helped me understand people better are my roles as certified coach and Master Practitioner in

Neuro Linguistic Programming. I have conducted retreats on life design and coached people to plan their present and future, helping them work through their deep sense of dissatisfaction and fear of changing directions.

I have to say an important skill I picked up is the art of listening (another by-product of my work interviewing people). You can listen in three ways: to defend, to align or to discover. You won't learn much if you're listening to defend unless it's an actual debate.

And if you listen to align so that the person thinks exactly like you, what would you learn? If everyone thinks like you, where is the excitement in that? It's more interesting to learn to discover and see different perspectives. Be thrilled when your perspectives change; it just means you have expanded your horizons.

One of the things I harp on in this book is the concept of delayed gratification. Some things take time and that's life. An ear of corn and an oak tree take different lengths of time to grow and such is life. Some things happen swiftly and others just take time to permeate and percolate. Sometimes you have to act on things immediately and sometimes you just have to smell the coffee while it's brewing.

It's not that I don't have a sense of urgency, I do. It's just that life has taught me some things don't go according to my plans and timings. I will be sharing some deep, dark secrets in this book ... ok, maybe not so dark but the harsh realities of life, like my father's death when I was 22 and my divorce not too long ago. These are not unique stories in the sense I'm not the only one who has experienced them, but one of the stages in the healing process is to talk about the experience. This isn't too commonplace in our part of the world.

Other things I will be addressing in this book: ageism, sexism, sizeism, you name it. Some of the beliefs we hold might indeed be holding us back. If you catch yourself saying things like "I'm too old for this" or "I'm too young for this", you've just put yourself in some self-imposed box. If there are deep-seated issues with body image (and show me one woman who hasn't experienced it), how do you look at and handle the situation? More importantly, how are you perpetuating that belief? If your gender biases have been holding you back, how do you overcome them?

Coaches have been crucial in my life. Having studied coaching, I know I need a coach too. There will be blind spots in our lives because we just can't see things ourselves. In fact, I have several coaches: from spirituality and fitness to life and business. These are investments in my life. I am also privileged to have had friend-tors in my life. Friends who uplift me and give insights into a whole slew of things.

My life has been a stage, literally. I have been given a visible platform which I have leveraged on and capitalised to expand my reach. I often ask myself why I have been given this platform. Nothing happens without a reason and as you read further, you will see that my entry into TV and radio has been both purely coincidental and dare I say it, divine. So given this opportunity, what can I do to influence and inspire others?

In the following pages, I will share some of the lessons that have left imprints on my life and how they have shaped me. The initial title of this book was "Defining Chapters", expressing how chapters in my life have defined and shaped me but at the same time (especially so for negative experiences), not defined me. You do have to admit the current title is more catchy.

If you have picked up this book, thank you. Thank you for taking the time (and spending the money) to read about my journey thus far. I hope you get at least a nugget of wisdom and maybe, this will save you the pain and/or money of making the same error. That said, I wouldn't change anything that has happened. The tapestry of my life wouldn't have been enriching and I wouldn't have had material to write about.

Every decade of my life is a different stage and has taught me lessons. I have dissected this book in these stages and maybe you'll see a little bit of yourself at different points of my life. Life is a stage, isn't it? While you're here, why don't you rock it? Welcome to my world.

" We can look at things from a scarcity or an abundance perspective. An abundance perspective means there is more than enough for everyone. And with that abundance, more abundance comes! "

STAGE 1

THE WONDER YEARS

On our annual family holiday back to Bau, a town about
40 minutes away from Kuching in Sarawak. Here I am about
four or five years old.

This is obviously the most difficult section to write, largely because I can't remember most of it. I have to say the first ten years of my life was definitely instrumental in laying the groundwork for my life. Education, family and friendships were the main foundations and I'm glad these have been solid.

I was born in Seria, Brunei. It was a different Brunei from the one now. At the time, it was a British protectorate and quite global since Seria was a Shell town. People who have grown up in oil townships know what I mean. I was born at number G11/27, a house which has since been torn down. In fact, all my siblings were born at home. My mum was a nurse and a midwife helped deliver us. I'm not sure if that was the norm then. Fortunately, all our births were normal and uncomplicated. I was the youngest of four children.

Growing up, I thought there was only one oil company in the world. Can you blame me? All our lives were dependent on this company in the town and the country. There were many perks growing up and I thought the whole world was this modern. My father worked for the company and when he got promoted to senior staff, we moved to a bigger home. I lived there throughout my life in Brunei. It was a beautiful house situated on an acre of land and someone came by to tend to the garden twice a week. Hot and cold water was easily available. The whole bungalow was fully air-conditioned. Most of my neighbours were from all over the world. Dutch, British,

Germans, Indians and a whole host of other nationalities lived in this oil town.

My father had a company car and we didn't have to pay for housing. We lived in front of the Panaga Recreation Club so I was there almost every afternoon either borrowing books or swimming. The sea was right behind the club and I often would swim there all by myself. If my own child did that now, I would freak out. But in those days, life was much more carefree.

Santa Claus, Christmas trees or any other decor in shopping malls during the Christmas season is not allowed in Brunei now. But back then, during Christmas, Santa Claus would arrive in a helicopter on the field of one of the recreation clubs. All the kids would go crazy as he passed out sweets and goodies.

Everything was five minutes away. My father started his day at 7am and some days he would take us to school, while other days, my mother did. My mother would take us back from school every day to home-cooked meals. My father finished work at 4pm and yes, in five minutes, he would be home, so I had plenty of quality time with him. The evenings would be spent with a bit of time in the garden followed by TV. There was hardly any homework and I made sure that was always out of the way before I went out to play. From climbing trees to examining whatever insects happened to be lying around, there couldn't be a better childhood.

School was a joy. I attended St. Margaret's School, which was started by missionaries in 1955. The medium of instruction was English with one subject in Bahasa Melayu, and we did the O-levels. It was a co-ed school, a fact I take for granted now. I remember the different nationalities in my school which included Gurkhas (Nepalese), Filipinos, Scots, English, Australians, Indians, Koreans and the locals. Looking back, meeting such a diverse group of people made a difference to how I viewed people. From learning to adapt and accommodate culturally, I learned that underneath our differences, we're all the same and want to fit in.

We went to school from Monday to Thursday, with Fridays off, and then back to school for half a day on Saturday. I had many fantastic teachers who enjoyed teaching. They were an eclectic bunch of teachers from India and the UK. One of them, Mrs Eileen McIntyre, made English enjoyable for me during the period when my parents moved away from Brunei and I was left behind. Once she took me out to the club because she saw from my essay that I was troubled about not having my parents around and dreading the impending move to Kuching. Life as I knew it was about to end and I was holding on to what was familiar to me, for as long as possible. I told her all these and from that day, she wasn't only a teacher but also a confidante. I don't think they make teachers like that anymore. We are still in touch today even though she lives in Spain now.

The choices of media included one local TV channel, Radio Television Brunei (RTB) and two channels from Malaysia, which were difficult to get hold of. When it came to radio, there was RTB and the British Forces Broadcasting Station (BFBS), which was only available in the Belait District. There were still British soldiers there then.

I enjoyed listening to the UK's *Top of the Pops* on radio plus a barrage of British TV shows. I think my humour must have been influenced a lot by British TV. There was no proper rating system so some were quite adult in nature, like Benny Hill with his raunchy humour. We also had a fair share of American classics and popular TV shows. *Sesame Street* was a staple growing up.

It really, really was a very small town. When I went back a few years back, my body went on automatic with all the road turnings and it seems nothing had changed. I could still automatically drive to the house where I spent my primary school years. It's nice to know that with some things, time has stood still and things remained unchanged. Yes, it was a very different Brunei then and I couldn't have asked for a more wonderful childhood.

Guilt Will Haunt You

From early on in primary school, I did well academically. I also developed a "kiasu" (don't want to lose) attitude and was determined to be No. 1 in class. Every term was an emotional roller-coaster ride for me on whether I would retain my position. I felt that if I just relaxed a little bit, someone else would be at my heels.

Along with my "kiasu" attitude, I also developed a bit of a bully complex with some followers in my clan. Yes, top girls do get noticed but maybe not for the right reasons. In Primary 3, this lovely girl from Singapore joined our class. Pauline Yow Pei Lian was sweet-natured, made friends easily, and had long, flowing hair. She was very good in her studies and teachers would notice her, especially when it came to art. I sucked at art.

Because I had these "leadership" qualities (I had not yet learned the lesson from Spider-Man: With great power comes great responsibility), I then decided to solicit the help of my clan to not befriend her. "Don't friend her," I told them. The poor girl didn't know what hit her.

Pauline would come to school wondering why no one was talking to her. I could see the sadness in her eyes. I don't know how long this went on for. Maybe a week, maybe two. And then one day, she just didn't come to school. After a few days, I asked everyone where she disappeared to. The teacher announced that she had gone back to Singapore as her father got transferred. I don't know if her father really got transferred or maybe they left because she was miserable in school.

It's been decades since that incident and I have tried looking for her online to ask for her forgiveness. She might have forgotten the incident but I haven't. It is something that still haunts me to this day.

As I look back on life, I believe we all have mean streaks in us. If we don't act on it, we most definitely think about it. Thoughts become words become behaviour become habits become values become your destiny, to paraphrase Mahatma Gandhi, who said:

"Your beliefs become your thoughts,
Your thoughts become your words,
Your words become your actions,
Your actions become your habits,
Your habits become your values,
Your values become your destiny."

Call it conscience or a prompting from God, I am glad my conscience was pricked. I am glad I was self-aware then to realise I don't like being that person. I can safely say that after that incident, I have never purposely been mean to someone for no reason. This is not to say I will not fight the good fight (though not in a physical sense) for causes I believe in or when I see injustice. I also believe in the good fight to improve myself.

If I see someone excelling in something, I then work at it and aspire to be better for myself, rather than for the sake of competing with anyone. The only competition is myself, to do my personal best in everything I do. However, to be mean is just to be mean. Self-reflection now shows me my own insecurities; in the past, to hide my own insecurities, I projected them onto someone else. Let someone else's success cause you be aspirational and not envious. I look at someone like Jennifer Lopez and think of her ability to be versatile and stay in the industry after so many decades, and how she has reinvented herself to be relevant to the times.

You don't have to look very far. I look at my friends with happy families and learn from them the formula for such close-knit relationships with husband and kids. I look at my fit friends and find out how they do it. We can look at things from a scarcity or an abundance perspective. An abundance perspective means there is more than enough for everyone. And with that abundance, more abundance comes!

In your words and actions, be a source of encouragement and kindness to others. It doesn't mean being a doormat. Some people can be draining; recognise that too. I am always available to listen to my friends. Most times I ask if they want my advice or do they just want me to listen. I have this conversation with my son too. And if they want advice, then I'll give it.

However, there are some people who gripe all the time and won't take advice. For self-preservation purposes, I choose to extricate myself from that situation lest I be taken down the same downward spiral. Direct people to the right place for advice if you feel you can't be of real help. That's the best thing because familiarity also builds contempt.

Back to the story of Pauline Yow, I have addressed the issue of guilt by forgiving myself for my bad behaviour so many decades ago. It is important that you do. However, if you have a conscience (and I hope you do!), guilt is not a good feeling. It robbed me of true joy for many years and caused me unnecessary anguish. I am self-aware of my bad behaviour, and do not want it to be part of my DNA.

Pauline Yow Pei Lian, if you ever read this, I hope you're living the life of your dreams. I don't know if you can remember the incident. I am truly sorry for my bad behaviour. Even though it happened in the last century, I still think about it. Please forgive me?

Life Lesson: Don't let guilt eat you. Seek forgiveness where possible. If not, forgive yourself and be kind to others.

Talents and Gifts

This only came back to me only recently. I can't remember why I forgot it. Looking back, the signs were there. Taking part in drama, debates and science contests, oratory skills came naturally for me. I didn't think of it as a "career". What? Acting? I came from a very, very small town in Brunei. The population of the country when I was born in was just over 100,000, so it was difficult to have a bigger vision than what I saw on TV.

My stage experience in school consisted of taking part in the school play one year when I played the lead role of the evil Queen Marguerite. There also was a national debate competition when St. Margaret's went up against St. George, one of the top schools in the country. We went to the big capital city of Bandar Seri Begawan and got to the finals of the debate. We fought the good fight but came in second place. I can't actually remember much of the details but I do remember the experience being fun and thrilling.

Now on to the Radio Television Brunei (RTB) story. I must have been around 11. The school announced that there was a national storytelling competition organised by RTB and I was chosen by the teacher to take part at the district level. I was nervous yet pleased I made it to the final rounds. Before going for the finals, my teacher took me aside and said, "Why don't you write your own story? Make it original and make it local. Everyone would be using some fairy tale so why don't you come up with an original story? That would make your story stand out from the rest." Like I wasn't pressured enough. A child can only handle so much.

I proceeded to write a story about a fire breaking out in Kampung Ayer, an iconic village in Brunei consisting of a cluster of stilted villages built on the Brunei River. The fire provided for great sound effects in the storytelling. There was also a hero who came to save the village. Maybe if I had written the story today, it would be a heroine!

On the day of the finals, I arrived at RTB and I had never been to a TV station before that. It was all quite a blur because all I could remember was my throat being very parched and me turning very pale. I was standing in front of an audience of perhaps a few hundred people. It felt like a million eyes were looking at me and all I wanted was to get it over and done with. So there I was shaking in my knees, reciting the story, hoping I wouldn't forget what I wrote. I remembered it being shorter than the other stories, but I was sure I had done my school proud already just by getting into the finals.

When it came to announcing the winners, I wondered why my name was not called. I dreaded going up on stage to collect the consolation prize. I waited. And waited. Why haven't they called my name? Suddenly, it came down to the Top 2. Wait. What? Top 2? Well, I didn't win the competition. I didn't think I would get that far.

First of all I was just relieved. And yes, genuinely happy. My parents were thrilled with their little girl. How did I forget about this experience until recently? Maybe because I thought it was just a one-off incident, a fluke. Who would have thought that many years down the road I would end up back in the radio station?

I now recognise that I enjoyed taking part in such activities and had a knack for communicating. It doesn't seem like a big deal. And sometimes people recognise these talents in you without realising it. Thank you for the teachers who saw something in me and encouraged me to participate.

Sometimes we suppress the things we are good at because we don't think there are career choices we can make with the things we love doing and are naturally gifted in. It was definitely the case for me growing up. I am glad my parents never stopped me from doing anything I loved. I believe parents now are more open to whatever their children want to do. The world is changing so fast and technology has changed the way we work and new business models are emerging every day.

I truly believe technology will only enhance the things we are good at and not destroy it. When you look back on your life, do you see a pattern or trend in things you enjoyed and did naturally well in? Maybe it's time to revisit those skills and see where you can pick up where you left off. Take some time out and list those things you found pleasure in as a child. It doesn't have to be a career change but maybe you can do some prototyping and experimenting with those lost skills and talents and see where they take you. Give it a shot!

That said, I believe in serendipity. How God will open doors for me in the most unexpected places and show you signs of where your skills and talents lie even from a very young age. And at the same time, not to rush things because things will run a natural course. As a hard-core planner, I plan for things and at the same time, I know the fruits of my labour will show up at the right time. Trust the system and trust the process.

Life Lesson: What are your skills and talents? What are you good at and what do you enjoy doing? What are you passionate about? Don't hide your treasures!

Always Be Learning

Is the love for reading nature or nurture? My early memory of being read to was by my older sister, Sylvia, when she played teacher and I was her willing student. I love the sound of words. I never got excited with toys or dolls but my eyes sparkled when I get a book. I loved getting a hardcover book; I loved all the colours and words and the smell of new books. My cousin Ilona would also spend her Sundays with us going to the only bookstore in town, where I could spend hours reading.

Moving to Kuching, Sarawak in Malaysia from Brunei meant having to part with my books and I still wonder what happened to those books. In the years that followed, I graduated to the Asterix and Obelix and the Tintin collections. My repertoire was wide. I even attempted romance novels for a while but that got tiring. In my twenties, my interest in novels waned and I got interested in personal development and autobiographical books. If I do buy books nowadays, they have to make me laugh and provide an escape. Life is serious enough.

There is so much wisdom in books. My attitude towards books (or people I meet generally) is this: I try to learn at least one thing from

Sylvia and I, at seven and three years old.

the author. There is always a nugget of wisdom, an "a-ha" moment. And so I read the book searching for it. People come with different maps of the world, with such unique perspectives and it always fascinates me to see how people think. The world is such an interesting place because of this.

Someone once said you can watch TV or listen to the radio and still be distracted or multi-task. However, when you pick up a physical book, your whole being is involved. Your eyes and mind are focused on every word. Sitting on the "throne" is not multi-tasking in this case!

Let me share some of the insights I have learned over the years. From the book *Personality Plus* by Florence Littauer, I worked out I had a Choleric personality, which although decisive in nature, can be a pain in the arse sometimes. I am still working on tapering it, especially when dealing with my son, who is generally a Phlegmatic personality and peaceful in nature.

The Five Love Languages written by Gary Chapman helped me identify my love languages of Quality Time and Physical Touch.

Again, these are not my son's love languages; I have to learn to speak in his love languages so that he knows he is loved. I can't just show my love in the way I know.

Mindset by Carol Dweck is about fixed and growth mindsets. The application of the mindsets from parenting to business has huge implications. I'll talk about that in another chapter. Dr Henry Cloud's series of books from *Necessary Endings* to *Integrity* hit me in a very practical sense on the kind of behaviours we have and more importantly, why we behave in certain ways. *Boundaries* for me was an eye-opener on why we are miserable in certain situations because we allow people to treat us in certain ways. The author likens it to letting thieves come into our house.

I go through different thought processes at different points in my life. Sometimes I buy a "What" book and this will be an understanding of a whole new topic. Or it could be a "How" book. This is when I want to know techniques, tips and strategies to do something. And when I am going through something in my life, I look for a "Why" book to get some collective wisdom from others. And you don't have to take everything as the gospel truth too. If you disagree with something, at least you're thinking about it. And that's a good thing!

These are just some of the books I have read. No, I haven't worked out all the answers and knowing these things doesn't mean I have perfected myself and no, there is no favourite book. Each brings with it its own unique offering. It starts with self-awareness, knowledge and then application of this knowledge, albeit very slowly in my case!

Charlie Tremendous Jones said: "You will be the same person in five years as you are today except for the people you meet and the books you read." I want the people I meet and the books I read to enrich and enhance me. I don't want to be the same person in five years' time. I want to be constantly evolving, growing and relevant. Don't you?

Electronic devices have made us turn away from reading. That said, if we can't beat them, join them. The recent Covid-19 pandemic has taught us many things. The working from home (WFH) phenomena changed the way people operate, hopefully for the better. Learning now may not necessarily be from books so please, invest in yourself and do some online courses which you can get from many sources like TED Talks to Masterclasses. These expand our horizon. Invest in 30 minutes a day. During the lockdown period, I went on LinkedIn Learning and learned about writing and how to think like a futurist.

We hear so much about Artificial Intelligence and Machine Learning. It is coming. Nay, it's already here. What does it mean to you? What does it mean for your children? How will it affect your livelihood? If there is one thing the Covid-19 pandemic has taught us, it is that there are many things that are beyond our control but there are still many things that are within our control. I always advise people to constantly upskill and reskill.

Stay in the present but keep your pulse on what's happening in the future. People always feel the rug being pulled out from under them, be it in relationships or career or health. Look at what's happening around you without the blinkers. Learn from people's mistakes and don't be caught off-guard. The inevitable will happen at times but at least know you're prepared as much as possible. There are no excuses.

As I am writing this, people are suffering pay cuts and job losses on a global scale because of Covid-19. Instead of being crippled by fear, do what you can to change the situation. You can make choices to invest in yourself. I have since this pandemic learned about developing an online course and conducting webinars and signed up for an online course in Design Thinking.

There is a saying: "There are three types of people – those who wonder what happened, those who watch things happen and those who make things happen. You decide which one you want to be."

Life Lesson: Make learning a lifelong habit. It comes in the form of books, audio materials, videos and the list goes on. There are no excuses if you want to stay relevant and active for the long-term.

Don't Have a Fixed Mindset!

As I was sharing earlier, I was constantly top of the class in school. When not checked, this can really feed your ego. I was fortunate to have parents who did not make a big deal of it. They were proud of me but they were never on my case to excel in my studies. It was always self-inflicted. I think that this was thanks to me being the youngest child out of four with a difference of nearly 10 years between my eldest brother and I – by the time my parents got to me, it was a case of, whatever goes!

I was in Primary 2 when my father submitted my results to the Chinese Club because they were giving awards out for top students. As it turned out, I had the highest average score and so I was given the "Best Of The Best" award. Can you just picture the head getting bigger? This was on top of the national story-telling competition on radio, getting picked to lead the parade for the Sultan's birthday and then being picked by my school to receive an award from Shell for Best Student – all before the age of 12. But then, when I went to secondary school and a bunch of students from the Chinese school turned up, I wasn't top in Maths anymore. Hell, I was beginning to lose understanding in Maths.

At around this time, my father received news that his contract would not be renewed. This short-circuited his plans for three years. My family went back to my dad's birthplace in Kuching and I stayed on in Brunei for a few more months with another family (who was not very nice) to finish the school year. That did not help with school at all. Oh yes, the hormones have also arrived. When you think you have reached your peak, that's when the danger begins.

Later, when I went to join my family in Kuching, I had to settle on a school which I didn't like and take on subjects that I was not interested in. I couldn't wait to get out of school. I accepted that I could not go to a local public university because I was educated in the English medium and schools in Malaysia were at that time taught in the national language, Bahasa Malaysia. I knew that a tertiary education was crucial, though I knew I couldn't afford an overseas education like all my friends who went off at 18. I knew I didn't want to do accounting, which almost all of my friends were doing. Constraints only make you more creative. And sometimes, necessity becomes the mother of invention.

So I went on my self-imposed gap year and took this opportunity to work as a receptionist in a hotel because I thought I would take up hospitality management. I spent that time doing research on courses and the validity and costs of these courses. Also, I wanted to see if I would enjoy this as a long-term career. During that period, I took up choral singing with the state choir. It paid pittance but I wanted to find out if there was an opportunity there too. I absolutely enjoyed learning the intricacies of choral singing and I think it helped me understand what went on behind voice control.

In that one year of self-reflection, I found a college that offered a twinning programme with a university in Australia offering a Bachelor's in Business degree. I could major in marketing (which was more interesting than accounting in my books, pun intended), which I thought would allow me to work in hospitality or almost any industry. The course also allowed me to do the whole degree in Malaysia and, if my parents could afford it, the option of spending the final year over in Australia.

After completing my course, there were new self-discoveries. I found out I excelled in advertising and public relations, things I never even heard of three years earlier. The whole world opened. I'll share about the rest of my journey in the chapters to come.

Many years on, I read *Mindset* by Carol Dweck and realised that I did have a growth mindset and not a fixed one. I am not sure if this is disposition or the fact that not everything came easy for me. I was not mollycoddled by my parents so I guess that helped too. They were not very educated so they had no expectations of me but only that they would support me to the best of their abilities.

If you have not read the book, I strongly suggest you do so or watch her TED Talk. She talks about the power of BELIEVING you can improve; the idea that we can grow our brain's capacity to learn and to solve problems. You naturally look for people who are worse than yourself to make yourself feel better. You see this in the working environment, where people put others down to make themselves better. It's called office politics.

People sometimes use age as an excuse not to learn or change. They say things like how you can't teach old dogs new tricks. Don't fall into that old adage if it doesn't serve you. I don't let mindsets like that determine my progress. No, you're never too old to learn; learn because you enjoy learning something new. I visually imagine new neurons forming in my brain when I am faced with something new. You don't know what you don't know and there's plenty I don't know. Isn't that exciting?

Fixed mindsets can happen in business, education, parenting and relationships. In the case of education, a bad result is not a death sentence. Nothing is really. We can learn, we can grow, we can change and we all have the capacity to improve.

When I look at my son now, I see that it's important to praise him. It's to praise wisely and to praise the process. Praise the effort, the strategy, the perseverance and not the result. It's dangerous when you think you've arrived because after that, what? Where is the reason to grow and change? Praise the progress and when you don't get something done, it's not the end, it just hasn't happened … yet.

Life Lesson: Always be learning and evolving. We're spoilt for choices on ways to learn. Take the step to learn something new.

Establishing Your Identity

Merriam-Webster describes identity as "the distinguishing character or personality of an individual". Initially I wanted to title this book "Defining Chapters", about the many defining chapters in my life, and how they didn't define me … or at least I didn't let them define me. Having a growth mindset, I believe things will happen in their time, so, as I said above, when something hasn't happened, it just hasn't happened yet.

When you are born in a country and grew up there, you think this is it, this is my life. I was born at home delivered by a matron. My mother was a nurse. Unfortunately the house I was born in has been torn down. My growing-up years were the best years ever. I am so glad I grew up in a small town. My father worked in Shell and would start work at 8am and leave work at 4pm. He would be home in 10 minutes.

I have fond memories of spending time with my father doing gardening and watching TV together. There was quality and quantity time. The air was fresh and everybody knew everybody. It was not a hectic city life like the one I live in now (a slow-paced life for grown-up me would suffocate) but it's great for a child.

So yes, I am grateful for my simple lifestyle and parents who were there for me. Children living in the city now are time-starved with extra classes and traffic jams. Why am I sharing my childhood story with you? Well, this was such a pivotal time of my life. You get anchored. You get anchored in your school, your friends, your family, your home and your country. The problem was, Brunei wasn't my country. For some odd reason, everyone in my family had permanent residence passes except me. No explanation whatsoever. So if my family wanted to stay on in this country, they could. And the moment I turned 18, I had to leave. I'll share more of that story later.

Why me? Connecting the dots which you can only do looking back (paraphrasing Steve Jobs here), God had closed the door for me there. Today, I cannot imagine living there and because of circumstances, that was never an option for a career for me. I've been back maybe twice since I left and I still shed a few tears flying in.

My last book was called *In Your Skin* and it was about being comfortable in our skin and defining success on your terms whether you're in sports or comedy or anything in between. The French expression is *être bien dans sa peau*. I look back and now think, what a colourful life I have led!

I am bringing this up because it is about discovering and forging my identity. Is my identity my personality, my character, my faith, my race, my nationality, my status, my job, my bank account, my looks or my body shape? When I first came back to Sarawak and then moved to Kuala Lumpur (living in Australia for a while in between), I could not connect with the country for a while because I didn't receive most of my education here.

My identity isn't about my nationality or my personality but it also is. We all have our own stories to tell and each of us can inspire. Our life's journey gives us our identity. The Japanese have a design philosophy called *wabi sabi*, where things made by hand are imperfect but it is this very thing that gives them their beauty and artisanal quality. The same is true for people. It is the combination of all of our imperfections that make us vulnerable and beautiful.

The Japanese also invented the art of *kintsugi*: repairing broken pottery by mending the areas of breakage with lacquer dusted or mixed with powdered gold, silver or platinum. As a philosophy, it treats breakage and repair as part of the history of an object, rather than something to disguise.

Most of us try to hide the imperfections. Embrace these moments. People are now craving for transparency, authenticity and grit. With Covid-19 happening around the world, it is the stories of people getting up again and again each time they fall that we relate to the best.

I wanted to start on this important point in the first 10 years of my life because that really set the foundation for the years to come. Every element of your life and every stage of your life helps in forging your identity. Be proud of what you've gone through in your life, at which ever stage you are.

Here's a story about my friend. "Maria" has had two marriages and the first thing she jumped into after the end of the second marriage was to get involved in another one. That relationship has since ended and she is miserable. She has said she tends to get involved with men who need to be taken care of. Knowing that, she is looking at jumping into another one. She's not taking time to love herself, thinking someone else will fill the void. Know your values and what you want in life. If it means taking time out, then so be it.

Think of those pivotal things that have happened in your life thus far: the good, the bad and ugly, and what you can learn from the situation and yourself. These things happen for a reason. Harvest and celebrate these lessons. Don't sweep it under the carpet. What do these incidents teach you and how can you be better from the experience? You don't want bad incidents to repeat itself because history has a way of repeating itself if you haven't learned the lesson.

Who knew the ensuing years for me would result in so many discoveries, fine-tuning, polishing, moulding and refinement? It's still ongoing. And you too have a story to tell. No one's perfect and that's perfection itself. What kind of strength and identity will you have if you haven't been through some highs and lows?

Life Lesson: Take the time to find out what your values are. Find three things you like people to say about you. Decisions in life are easier if you know what's important to you.

Sharing my fifth book, *In Your Skin*, with the Asia School of Business. The book is about how we need to be comfortable in our skin and determine what is success to us, and no one else.

STAGE 2

THE CONFUSED YEARS

My almost-18-year-old son has basically lived in the same home all his life. Aside from his parents' divorce more than eight years ago, he has had a relatively stable upbringing, raised by my ex-mother-in-law and I. He doesn't have to worry about food or money. He's now at a stage where everything is an excuse for an argument.

My always baby, Jude, at his high school graduation.

And so I am reminded of myself and my troublesome teenage years. I lived in three places in this decade: Seria, Kuching and Kuala Lumpur. My father's early retirement resulted in us making an unexpected move to Kuching, Malaysia to finish secondary school, jobs as a receptionist at Kuching Hilton and a part-time choral singer before heading to Kuala Lumpur and then finishing my final year of university in Toowoomba, Queensland.

Every decade shapes us, whether we like it not. Actually, every day can shape and refine us if we let it. And we can choose

Can you spot the angry teenager? I was around 16 at the time.

to learn from every stage in life. For the longest time I regretted some decisions like choosing to stay in Brunei to finish Form 2 instead of heading to Kuching with my parents and choosing the wrong school in Kuching. I now understand that these were the best decisions I could make with the available information at the time.

My heart aches for children in unstable home environments when I imagine how they make it through life. Although money was not scarce in our home, it was also not abundant. I always had food on the table so I was grateful. The home environment was smooth, considering the various moves. I also know now that with constraints, I am more resourceful.

One of the most significant decisions I made was taking a gap year. At that time, that was a foreign concept in these parts of the world. It is still a strange concept now for many Asian parents. A gap year is not an all-expenses-paid holiday! It's a year to do something else while figuring out what to study. Most parents I know are eager to churn their kids out to finish their studies and join the workforce as quickly as possible. Most times kids go through the rigamarole and emerge still confused after graduation.

And even after you graduate, you don't necessarily have to follow a particular path. My career path has not been straightforward but it's been built upon the foundation of my degree. The world has changed so much and you can get a formal education in so many ways now. University is still educational in terms of living on your own, budgeting, learning teamwork when working on projects, the friendships you make and the networks you build.

My gap year was spent working and earning money as a receptionist and a choral singer while figuring out what I wanted to study. The timeout gave me clarity and the chance to save some money for further studies. I probably enjoyed Kuching more after that and came to terms with that fact that this was my new hometown. Working made me grow up a little bit so by the time I went to Kuala Lumpur, I was a little bit more mature at 18 going on 19. It was a compact year because I also joined the Sarawak Symphony Orchestra as a choral singer.

In design thinking, a prototype is defined as a first or preliminary version of a device or vehicle from which other forms are developed. Now, if we consider our lives as prototypes, always think of everything you've tried as a preliminary version which is continuously improved.

We get so confined and defined by what we studied or the labels our friends and family members put on us. We can avoid this with a few reframes like "I am going to live out my fullest potential and see what resonates with me" or "What's the best that can happen if I try something new? I learn new skills."

We're not trees or static beings. If something is not working, do something about it. Any movement is a step forward. It's not the end of the world. At IBM, I took on six roles in 11 years. There was one year when I took on a role I didn't enjoy because it involved a lot of calculations. It was a year of finding out what I didn't enjoy but at the same time I learned a lot about processes. And it was thanks to that job being not suitable for me that I took the next step to look for something else. One door closes, another one opens!

The wonder years for me meant I spent many years wondering about my future, wondering what's going on around me with hormones raging and at the same time, the wondrous experiences I had packed in those short 10 years. May we all live in a state of wonderment forever, with a sense of naivety, innocence and the thrill of not knowing what's going to happen around the corner.

Regardless of how old I am, I always say my frame of mind is 19. Why? I had just come out to Kuala Lumpur to further my studies and this time I was really living on my own. A far cry from all the small towns and cities I had lived in until then, Kuala Lumpur is the capital and it was a much rowdier place then. Bright lights and big city, how do I navigate this labyrinth? How do I make my mark in this new home?

I was starting my university studies majoring in Marketing on a twinning programme with HELP University and the

University of Southern Queensland. I was so excited about my future after getting my degree; that was my first dream. That sense of awe, surprise and wonderment is still the frame of mind I like to be in. I want to live in that state as much as possible. "What am I going to learn and experience today?" What an enjoyable world to live in; to wake up every day with a sense of adventure.

Build Each Other Up

Remember that story I shared of how I was mean to Pauline Yow Pei Lian at nine years old? Well, karma has a way of biting you in the behind. Maybe God wants me to really learn the lesson. So, I was 13 going on 14, and my parents had gone to Kuching and I was staying with this family in Brunei, a couple with two kids, to finish out Form 2.

So there I was missing my parents, not doing too well at school and not liking it at "home". Fortunately I had a bunch of girlfriends, Wendy, Josephine and Emily, who were there for me during this troubled period. We had been friends for about seven to eight years by then.

It was the middle of the year and I had gone to Kuching to be with my parents for a few weeks. It was nice to be in Kuching and to get acquainted with this place which would be my new home in the future. After the few weeks were over, I went back to Brunei and suddenly ... none of the girls were talking to me! I had no idea why. Déjà vu on how I treated Pauline Yow Pei Lian in Primary 2!

This went on for weeks or months. As if I wasn't miserable enough. I couldn't even remember why they weren't befriending me. I think it was probably close to the end of the school year when they started talking to me again. I don't remember a major explanation. To this day, we are still in touch thanks to social media, though we're not close because two of them moved to Canada and another to Australia.

Maybe this whole episode is the way the Universe conspired for me to really understand the lesson of being nice and kind (Yes God! I get it!). Fast forward to the working world: in every job I have had, I have encountered mean people. People who would purposely chide you in public, backstab you to make themselves look better and manipulate situations to put you down.

I will share one experience when I worked on a proposal until late at night and only one other colleague was with me. I printed the proposal and left it on my desk so that it would be ready in the morning. When I arrived at the office the next morning, I found that the proposal had "mysteriously" disappeared and so I asked my colleague if she saw it. She feigned innocence. Of course I had to quickly print another set. How juvenile, you would say. Yes, I would agree.

In the course of work, I have also worked with people who were envious of my success and would work hard behind the scenes to sabotage me and my career. Dr Henry Cloud mentioned in one of his books that there are three types of people you will meet: the wise, the foolish and the evil. I'm going to paraphrase him.

Wise doesn't mean smartest, brightest or most talented. While wisdom may coexist with these traits, having wisdom means many things. It comes from experience, and to let experience do its work, a person has to be open to receiving the lessons that it has to teach. But the bottom line with a wise person is that they're open to feedback. Feedback helps the wise, and they value it. If a person is willing to take feedback, you will likely get your return on investment.

If the chief descriptor of the wise person is that when the light shows up, he looks at it, receives it, joins it and adjusts his behaviour to align with the light, the fool does the opposite: he rejects the feedback, resists it, explains it away and does nothing to adjust to meet its requirements. He's never wrong; someone else is.

When you deal with an evil person, you have to go into protection mode, not helping mode, and it's a big step to realise that there are people who hurt you because they want to. There are some people whose desire is to hurt others and you have to protect yourself with lawyers, guns and money.

You should talk to wise people about problems, talk to fools about consequences and not talk to evil people at all, period. You cannot deal with all people in the same way, but once you learn the character traits that give real reason to hope that they can be different, you can know better whom you want to invite into your tomorrow.

Ok, rather than stew and be bitter about things, what do I do instead? I usually take the negative energy and turn it into positive energy. Think about it, everything emits energy. If I focus on these situations, I would be more miserable. So instead, I take this energy and turn it into something positive.

Think of the windmill. Without the windmill, there is just wind blowing everywhere. However, with the windmill, all that energy is harnessed and channeled in the right direction. In the case of all that energy, I choose to channel it and use it to make something positive. Like writing this book for example. This is my sixth book so can you imagine where all that energy came from? Try not to laugh!

I always wonder why people are mean. I always feel that if people were mean to someone, the root cause is insecurity. Where does this insecurity come from? The mindset that there is scarcity as opposed to abundance. Abundance means there is more than enough for everyone and I truly believe that. Do you only listen to songs from one singer or one band? Do you only read one book from one author? Is there a lack of water in this world? Seventy percent of the world is covered in water. It is access to clean water which is the issue. So really, there is abundance in the world.

One of my mentors is Nancy Dornan, founder of Network 21, and she would say, "When you wake up in the morning, you wake up you and they wake up them." Simple yet so profound. Or as Michelle Obama said, "When they go low, you go high." There really is a better view the higher you go. I do not want to waste energy or headspace on negativity.

Madeleine K. Albright, former US Secretary of State, famously said, "There is a special place in hell for women who don't help other women." I think this applies to humankind as a whole. The recent Coronavirus pandemic showcased just that. We're all so interconnected. We're so small and yet we're so significant. Everything we do impacts everyone around the globe. Ponder on that for a moment.

There are things that are beyond our control but the mind is in our complete control. One of the most inspirational women I know, Arianna Huffington, shared this lesson from her mother when faced with a bad situation: "Just change the channel. You are in control of the clicker. Don't replay the bad, scary movie." The clicker is in our control. How powerful is that!

Negativity clouds your judgement. Negativity curbs creativity and innovation. Buddha said, "Holding onto anger is like drinking poison and expecting the other person to die." It is NOT easy, I know that. We're only human, but try to remember that when something negative happens.

Folks, we can all do our part. Build each other up. Karma has a way of showing up and life happens, so as much as possible, we can have a positive impact on every one we meet with the words we say and the goodness we are all capable of.

Life Lesson: Learn if you're dealing with the wise, the foolish or the evil. Never seek vengeance though, it's a waste of unnecessary energy. Build people up at every possible moment. It's a reflection of you, not the other person.

Prototype Your Life

I finished my O- and A-levels both at the same time. It was a private school and I wanted to speed things up. No, I didn't score fantastically. I decided to take some time off before deciding what I wanted to do next. If I haven't mentioned this already, Kuching is also a small town, though much bigger than Seria, Brunei where I spent the first 14 years of my life. There was one major international hotel in Kuching at that time, Holiday Inn.

So when news broke that another international hotel chain, the Hilton, was starting operations in Kuching, the whole town must have applied. I sent in my application because I had thoughts of taking up hospitality management at that time. I remembered the first round of selection was sitting for an English test. It was easy in my books.

I was thrilled when I was shortlisted and there I was doing my first interview. There were all these 17-year-olds fresh from finishing Form 5. I can't remember how long the interview took but voila, I got my first job as a receptionist. My salary was pathetic. There was no way I could survive if I didn't live with my parents. With my salary though, I did contribute to the electricity bills so yes, quite proud of myself. Thank goodness staff meals were provided when we were on duty and having a uniform meant saving on clothes!

At the same time, I heard from my colleague's father that the state was looking at setting up a choral team, the Sarawak State Symphony Orchestra (SONS). The choral master turned out to be my father's childhood friend although that's not why I got the part! We had practice sessions three times a week and were paid a tiny amount but the experience was invaluable.

I also had a Christmas gig when I was on school holiday. A Japanese restaurant called Kikotei was looking for performers. It was a three-piece with a violinist, violist and a keyboardist. I was by no means a talented musician but I could play three chords on the keyboard sufficiently well and that was probably my first paid gig.

When I came out to Kuala Lumpur to study, I saw an advertisement in the newspaper seeking a part-time deejay in a discotheque in one of the hotels. No experience required because the main deejay was willing to teach. So on Friday and Saturday evenings, I would catch a bus to the hotel and work until about 1am or 2am and get a fixed taxi driver to take me home after. It was fairly decent pocket money for a 19-year old! Eventually I knew I didn't want a job that went on late into the night. But being behind the console was an experience in learning to be comfortable on a stage.

This lasted for all of three months when I worked for two nights a week over the weekend. It got tiring after a while and I really had to concentrate on my studies. No, my parents never knew about this job. So all of these varied experiences before I turned 20!

Why am I sharing this with you? If I looked back at those adventures, I had a lot of fun. I didn't think if anything was going to be a major career move but all the things I did back then did help with my confidence and skill sets. So nothing was a waste of time. Working as a receptionist taught me people skills, whether it was with guests or colleagues. I also learnt the inner workings of an international hotel chain.

Singing with the choir helped train my voice and although I don't sing on radio, I learned about voice control and it was just joyful and magical when we all got together to sing. We sang for the state governor, and also the king of Malaysia. Standing on stage was intimidating but thank goodness, we had a whole load of people on stage together! I learned about all sorts of musicals from *The Sound of Music* to *South Pacific*. It was just pure bliss after each practice session alone.

At one Christmas performance with about 20 to 30 people having their Christmas eve dinners, no one was really paying attention or applauding. Granted I was there for the money. The lesson learned was that you just had to get the work done whether anyone applauds you or not. That was my first paid appearance on stage. I also learned that I was not a talented musician, but I thank my parents for music lessons growing up. Their ROI (return on investment) was never fully recouped, unfortunately!

These are all building blocks to future experiences. These were skill sets used in my work in the future. Everything interconnects. In the study of design thinking, a prototype is defined as "a simulation or sample version of a final product, which is used for testing prior to launch." The goal of a prototype is to test products (and product ideas) before spending lots of time and money into creating the final version of the sellable product.

Now why can't we treat life like a prototype? If one idea doesn't work, try another one. Experiences and knowledge is never wasted. We learn another idea that doesn't work ... but what if it does? That famous analogy by Thomas Edison: He didn't fail 10,000 times in inventing the light bulb, he found 10,000 ways in which it wouldn't work. Thank goodness he persevered, otherwise we would be sitting in the dark.

A while back I took a writing course although I had published my first book already. I wanted to improve my writing style. We were given all sorts of exercises to incite creativity. One of them was drawing and to write about our drawing. To say it was an eye-opener would be an understatement. Another friend who took the writing course found out she could draw and paint very well from doing that exercise and now she's an advertising executive turned artist. How fantastic is that!

I have also found that it has been fun trying out different types of things and enriching my life in so many ways. What will be your next prototype?

Life Lesson: Life is an adventure. Try different things because it expands you mentally and sometimes physically and financially too!

Survival of the Adaptable

As I'm writing these stories and reflecting on the first 20 years of my life, my move from country to country and town to town had such a profound impact on me. It wasn't a case of the survival of the fittest but the ability to adapt. It was such a pain looking back but it definitely helped with my figurative backbone.

Let me rewind to that time when I went to Kuching at 14. For all my years in Brunei, I was in a co-ed school and my medium of education was English. When I moved to Kuching and it was time to register for school, I had choices to make. I was offered a spot at the top school there, a girls' school with the medium of education in the national language, Bahasa Malaysia. Although I know the language because it was taught in Brunei, it was not what I was used to.

My parents – bless their hearts – decided to let me make my own decision when it came to my education. I decided to go to a private missionary school (no, not one of those fancy ones). I skipped a class so that I could continue in the English medium.

I spent three years in that school which I absolutely hated. I crammed for the O- and A-levels and also did some subjects with the London Chamber of Commerce Industry (LCCI) qualifications body. The aim was to get out. What were the changes I was experiencing? Puberty was one! Also, having to make new friends was tedious.

The school was highly religious and strict and all I wanted to do was rebel. I was always looking for ways to beat the system or bend the rules. Basically just silly juvenile and delinquent behaviour.

I wasn't doing too well in school but I knew the importance of getting an education. My mind was whirring on how I could get out of the situation. I had already opted for a route that would not allow me to get into public universities, but that wasn't a goal anyway. I also resented my parents for letting me make my own decisions. How was a 14-year old to know the right pathway for her future? Career counsellors were not that well known then. My parents were not that educated so couldn't advise and they always trusted me to make the right decisions. It was just everything that came along with it like puberty, missing friends and leaving my birthplace, knowing I would never return to it again.

For a long time, I actually resented my parents for not being able to lead me better. I felt angry that I had to decide on the school and wondered why life wasn't easier. Now that I have grown up, I understand that they loved me and did all they could to the best of their ability and knowledge. I know that I never had to miss a meal and I was clothed, sheltered and loved.

Many people like to blame the situation and other people for their predicament. I like this quote from Jim Rohn: "Don't wish it was easier, wish you were better. Don't wish for less problems, wish for more skills. Don't wish for less challenge, wish for more wisdom." Isn't that a better mantra in life?

How do I prepare for the new normal? The global pandemic called Covid-19 got all of us on our knees. You know what? I think what happened in my teenage years prepared me somewhat for the future. Change is constant. There will be uncertainty always.

"It is not the strongest of the species that survives, nor the most intelligent, but the one more responsive to change." This quote from Charles Darwin, the father of evolution, is a particularly helpful reminder for anyone who lacks the confidence to go out and pursue their dreams.

I sometimes think what my life would be like if everything went as planned. That is, I finish Form 5 in Brunei and go overseas to study straight after. Would I be less of a risk-taker in life generally because everything was laid out so easily?

People talk of the younger generation today as the "strawberry generation" because they bruise easily and are less resilient. I don't think it's a case of generation but more upbringing and privilege. So I wonder if I would bruise easily too.

And when I look at how things have panned out in my life, this series of events connects. Maybe it's also my perspective, mindset and view of these things. I think because of all these events, it has helped shape me on my view of life. I knew from a young age that there was no such thing as job security, health is crucial, as are being independent and open to new experiences.

The Serenity Prayer is a prayer written by the American theologian Reinhold Niebuhr. It is commonly quoted as: "God, grant me the serenity to accept the things I cannot change, courage to change the things I can, and wisdom to know the difference."

In life, there are things that you can control and influence and some things you can't. When you recognise that, it makes life clearer. Like the pandemic that is happening now, I can't control it but I can control my attitude towards it and things I can do despite it. Also trust that when you have made decisions, that these were the best decisions with all the knowledge you had at that time. Don't look back and wish you had done something else. Trust that you made the right decision at that time.

When you have no control of the situation, can you have influence over the situation? The Movement Control Order (MCO) in Malaysia because of Covid-19 has taught me things I can do despite not being able to move around. First of all, I turned to online learning. I learned new things like journal therapy and design thinking and areas of growth opportunities. There is plenty of free material around.

I made sure I exercised every day. For someone who is used to exercising outdoors, this was a culture shock of sorts. So I swept the patio, which gave me some much-needed sun. I looked for exercise videos I could do indoors and made sure 10,000 steps were achieved. I participated and conducted webinars. I started writing this book with a simple goal of 1,000 words a day. I learned about new technological tools available. I looked at future ways of monetisation so that should something like this happen again, I will be better prepared. I celebrated every small win.

Exercise is key to getting the happy hormones going naturally.

And to this day, I still like my routines and my set ways of doing things. We are all creatures of habit at the end of the day. I am grateful though that when something unusual happens, I've had prior experience! And some days, when I'm feeling extra brave, I'll actually say, "Bring it on!"

Life Lesson: Be adaptable. It's actually a growth mindset and not something that cannot be done. Take a micro step of doing something different today even if it's just 15 minutes.

Constraints Result in Creativity

When I was about eight, I had grand ambitions to be a doctor. I don't know where that came from. The parents never encouraged or discouraged me in that direction. Fortunately, I came to my senses even before I had to decide whether to go to the arts or science stream, and decided that medicine was not for me.

And I knew it wasn't the question of intellect but interest and what I was geared to to do. I always tell my son, recognise your strengths, gifts and talents and therein lies the clue of what you'll naturally be good at. That said, you need to work on those talents. We've heard stories of artists and sports people who didn't work as hard as the next person. Anyway, I digress.

I shared earlier how I took that one productive year (self-imposed gap year and didn't know it was called a gap year then) working as a receptionist in Kuching Hilton and moonlighting as a choral singer in the evenings, trying to decide my future. It was very empowering and liberating receiving my first pay cheque, miniscule as it was.

My father at this time had already retired. There was no pension to speak of except savings. Also, the options for public university were not open to me because I did not go through the local education system. My friends and peers were going overseas and so I was envious and resentful.

My end objective was to get an overseas education. My first preference was the UK and the second option was Australia. I knew I didn't want to do accounting, finance, economics or law. My cousin who was a mature student told me about marketing and that was quite interesting in my books.

Let me paint you the educational scenario in Malaysia in the 1980s and 1990s. Other than going overseas, a lot of private colleges were offering twinning programmes in Kuala Lumpur. It was mostly a case of one year in Malaysia and two years overseas in the popular courses I talked about. They were all still outside my parents' budgets. I didn't have to ask.

So I scoured the newspaper daily for new colleges that would be offering alternatives. Yes, it was life before the Internet. I spotted an advertisement for a fairly new college. They were accepting students with all sorts of qualifications and they had tied up with an institute of higher education in Queensland, Australia. Mind you, most of my peers were heading to either Sydney and Melbourne at that time.

I checked out the college and they offered marketing in addition to the usual majors. And it allowed me to do the whole course in Malaysia or go over to Australia if I chose to and could afford to. I was intrigued! Now it came to the course fees. It was half the price of the other places. Next would be convincing the parents because it meant having to move to Kuala Lumpur too and that would incur costs. Sarawak later hosted two Australian universities that set up campuses there. Only 10 years after I was college hunting, of course!

Thankfully, my parents agreed and I had the opportunity of getting an Australian education even if I didn't go to Australia. The end story of that educational journey was that I did get to go to Australia for my final year. Boy, I was glad I did because it opened up my eyes to so many things. I got to do a marketing degree which I completely enjoyed. It was in that final year in Australia that I discovered this subject called public relations, which became a career path for me for a good part of my working life.

The last picture taken with my parents before heading to Australia to study.

I think if my parents couldn't afford it, I would still go to Kuala Lumpur to work and study part-time anyway. The opportunities were there. What did the whole experience teach me? It taught me to be patient, to persevere and to research. So the path to my end-goal was not so straightforward but not a lot of people can say they worked in a hotel and did choral singing!

If you have a goal, you'll get there in the end. It is only when there are constraints that we get creative and solution-oriented. In the business scenario, no great idea ever came about with unlimited resources of funds and manpower. It is only when there are limits and restrictions that people get creative.

Celebrate it when things don't come so easy. This is a test if something really matters to you. If it doesn't, then so be it, but if it does, you will find a way. We are all resourceful people and resources may not mean money. It's the easiest solution if money can be thrown in to solve a problem. It's a test of your mettle, innovativeness and creativity when you solve an issue. When you see an obstruction in your way, you can get over it, under it or through it. Your resourcefulness will show you how.

Now as much as I don't like roadblocks and obstacles like every other human being, treat them as blessings. You'll find out other things about yourself in the process. "Life is what happens to you while you're busy making other plans." This famous saying from John Lennon reflects a paradox in our lives. Lennon doesn't say we shouldn't make plans, but that the true experience of being alive is beyond those plans, and "happens" to us. As I've grown older (and wiser), some things just take time to percolate and we just have to live in the present.

Life Lesson: When things come in your way as a hindrance to your progress, change your words and instead of saying "Oh no!" ask yourself, what are three things I can do to overcome this?

No Such Thing As Soul Mates

Back to Kuching when I was 14 years old. It was time to make new friends in this new town I had to call home now. I had new classmates and there was your usual mix of boys and girls. There was this boy in class whom I shall call Tom (because I like Tom Hiddleston). We would talk a lot but I don't think I felt for him in any way. We were good friends and just liked talking to each other. Tom and I sat in front of the class maybe because we were talking so much.

One day, he didn't turn up for class and when he turned up the next day, I said "I miss you", not in a romantic way but in a friendly way. I think it was not too long after that that we just looked at each other in class during a break and we held hands. Something happened that day that I don't think I'll ever experience again. You never forget your first love really.

This went on for the rest of the school year and then suddenly as he entered Form 5, he said we should stop seeing each other because he had to focus on his exams. He said he loved me and that he'd come back again when he was "settled" in life. How dare he be so responsible? My heart broke. Yes, you can actually feel physical pain when your heart breaks. I must have cried every night for three months.

My heart turned cold after that. I vowed never to let anyone hurt me again. He left for Australia the year after Form 5. I must have pined for him for years. I would find his address and write to him every so often. He never replied. It was just as well that he broke up with me because I really had to focus on my studies. I didn't though.

About three years later, I received this letter in my mail. The handwriting looked familiar. When I opened the letter and saw that it was him, I burst out crying again. I had gone out with other guys by then but no one could quite replace him and maybe I did put him on a pedestal.

He wrote that he was coming to Kuala Lumpur and would like to meet up. Boy was I excited! Yes, we did meet up in Kuala Lumpur and he told me 'he was going to graduate soon. He never went out with anyone else and was hoping that, when he graduated, we could take up where we left off. Guess what? I cared for him immensely but realised I didn't feel like that for him anymore.

I had moved on. I wished I hadn't but I had. He was and is a sweet fellow and is still one of the kindest people I know. I am glad he was my first love because it is proof that there are wonderful and respectable men out there who genuinely care for women. He never took advantage of me at all.

When people talk about "soul mates" or needing someone to complete you (as popularised by romantic movies), it's not true. I do believe you can meet someone who has the same values as you, such as commitment, integrity and loyalty or whatever that matters to you personally. The danger of similar interests is short-lived. What excites you in your twenties won't excite you as you get older. Why? We go through life stages: being single, being married, having children and the list goes on.

If you use values as your benchmark and work towards setting goals as a couple, that will take you further. How often have we heard of people drifting apart? When that happens, it means that relationship was based on a weak foundation. Allan Pease, who has written over 15 books on communication, said that many times we set goals for ourselves and forget to set goals as couples. When we don't do that, we will drift apart. Differing interests and values will make it challenging to stay together.

The point of all this is that relationships are complicated and as painful as it may seem at that time, it really isn't the end of the world. Let go of the notions of the stuff Hollywood movies

(Bollywood and Korean for that matter) make romance out to be. I am not a sceptic and still believe in having someone special in my life. I also believe that it takes work for anything to work.

The first few years of romantic life is when oxytocin is high in men, so they are extra loving and testosterone is high in women, so they are more sexually active. And then things pan out. This is when the test of real love comes into play. When it gets beyond eros love. Eros is one of the four ancient Greco-Christian terms which can be rendered into English as "love". The other three are storge, philia, and agape. Eros refers to passionate love or romantic love; storge to familial love; philia to friendship as a kind of love; and agape refers to selfless love. When your love for your spouse transcends all four, then that to me is real love.

As much as my first love has had such an impression in my life, I know it's not the be all and end all that it did not work out. Our souls are not connected. Imagine if we believed in the fallacy of The One and that person should pass away, what then? There are options out there and I strongly believe when it's time, it's time.

So enjoy and cherish the time you had with your first love. That cannot be taken away and hopefully you had a happy, memorable one. Take it for what it is: a wonderful memory. If you are fortunate enough to still be with your first love, kudos to you. I am sure a lot of hard work and adjustments have been put in to get you where you are today. This hard work and perseverance will be a lifetime commitment too.

By the way, did I mention my first boyfriend and the ex-husband were both Wongs? Two Wongs don't make a right! Couldn't resist that.

Life Lesson: No one completes you. You complete yourself. Only when you are whole, will you meet someone equally whole.

STAGE 3

THE ESTABLISHING YEARS

I want to address childbearing concerns first of all. Most people, though not all, would be thinking about children, even if it's just at the back of their minds. With the twenties and thirties being the most productive years to have children, I believe we are consciously and unconsciously thinking about finding a mate. This didn't occur to me because at 23, I had already met the man I was going to marry and have children with. It was something that was ticked off on the checklist.

Most women would be thinking about a lot of things at this stage: career, money, finding a mate, buying a house, having a baby and all the worldly concerns. I know that things have changed in the last few decades but I would safely say that these would be the key concerns. A man, on the other hand, doesn't have the biological clock to think about. When younger women come to me for advice, I always say, have your eggs frozen if you can afford it. It helps to take something off your mind for many years if you're concerned about building your career or if the partner to help you in that journey hasn't come along yet.

For most people, their twenties would be spent carving out their career. It certainly was the case for me. After graduation, I was in two minds about which career path I wanted to take. Looking back, it wouldn't have been a death sentence if I did either but eventually I decided on PR. I wanted to work for an international PR consultancy.

PR at that time was a fairly new industry and I wanted to learn the tricks of the trade before joining a particular vertical industry. I was fortunate I managed to get a job at Edelman PR. This was the 1990s and Malaysia was booming. After working for just a year, I started getting job offers left, right and centre. Yet somehow I knew I wasn't ready with the knowledge and tools of the trade yet. It's so easy to look at friends moving on to new jobs with amazing pay raises but still I resisted. The concept of delayed gratification was not new to me although I didn't know the expression then. I wanted to be really good at my role and believe the right job with the right money would come along when I was fully ready.

It took about five years before I finally felt ready to move, and I joined IBM. It was a choice between joining the IT or pharmaceutical industry. I felt both had potential and I genuinely enjoyed working on these sort of accounts. Truth be told, one of the reasons I joined IBM was also proximity to where I lived.

With the girls at Edelman PR in my early twenties.

So my twenties were spent establishing myself career-wise, relationship-wise and on the home front. The career, the relationship, the car, the insurance and the home. Is that what people still do nowadays? Whether people want to buy homes and cars now is debatable.

I look at the cost of homes now and I wonder how people can even get started. However, do think of flipping: when you buy something that's more affordable then flip it for something bigger when you're more financially able. There is the power of compounding, the earlier you save. And when you buy the home, you will feel it takes forever to pay the mortgage. Looking back, I am so glad I made the decision to tighten the belt and suffer then than to suffer now.

The other thing to look at is insurance. You don't want to be left in the lurch and have all your savings depleted should you ever need the funds. It's also cheaper when you're younger. Make sure you get a medical card too. I got additional insurance even when I was working at IBM which had great insurance and hospitalisation benefits.

Most of my investments were spent on self-improvement. This was an investment until today because the best person to invest in is yourself. Time goes by very quickly. Really in the blink of an eye, life happens. And although life does happen to you when you're busy making plans, plan anyway.

Although I think I have more energy now than I have ever had, physiologically you do have more energy in your twenties and thirties. Due to the right choices I made earlier, I have more options now. I managed to buy two homes during the time I was married and in the worst case scenario, I have an extra home to sell. I am putting this simplistically. I know because I made some right choices when I was in my twenties, I had more choices in terms of career changes and travel in my forties.

I only wish I took my investment in my health and fitness more seriously. There are more complications as you get older and although I am fortunate in terms of health, it is a lot more difficult to shed excess weight the older you get. In my younger days, I practised a lot less self-care or self-love. I didn't even go for facials or massages thinking these were a waste of time and money.

Do I regret not going on as many holidays? Well firstly, I didn't have as much disposable income but I still managed a holiday a year. They were mostly short ones but it was always a dream to be able to afford the fancy holidays. Boy am I glad that social media like Instagram and Facebook were not available then. I am sure I would have developed holiday envy!

If there was a time for you to invest in yourself, your twenties would be a great time to set foundations financially, whether it is for a career or business. It's never too late to start anything later in life but the twenties is a great time to experiment a little bit more when there are less commitments like children. That said, this shouldn't be a time to ignore all aspects of your Wheel of Life. No point being successful in your career to find out all your friends have disappeared.

I held two jobs at the time. That was the reality and that was the hustle. I rented a cheap room and only bought my first car after working for two years. It was one of my proudest moments because I earned it on my own. Hard work and diligence never killed anyone. It did mean my weekends were spent working and not so much socialising. Again, delayed gratification over instant gratification.

If you were to design your life, here are some questions for your consideration. I wished I had asked these questions when I was younger. Also, review it yearly, every 10 years or when a life situation has changed, like a new job or a new baby.

Firstly, it's about creating your vision for your life. Your vision, not anyone else's. Not the "I want to lose 10 pounds" kind of vision but an overarching vision of your life. What kind of person are you? Where do you live? What do you do for a living? How do you dress? How do you make others feel? How will you travel? What are the top three things that need to happen in order to start making that vision a reality? Once you've identified the three things, dissect each goal with three action steps and a timeline. And really, start with only three goals. Don't overextend yourself or you will overwhelm yourself.

Secondly, it's about defining success. What does success mean to you? Where did you learn this definition? Are you successful? Why? If not, what would it take for you to get there? When have you felt successful in the past? What led to that success? Who were you when that success happened? Who helped you win? Who are some successful people you admire? What are the qualities about those people that you like? Answering these questions will give you greater clarity.

And if there are areas you would like to improve, try one area first. What is the one area of your life you'd like to be successful in? What will it take to get you there? What qualities, skills and talents do you have now that will help you be successful? What new skills do you need to acquire? What else can you learn? What do you need to leave in the past? Write a personal mantra about success.

Take the time to do this exercise!

Don't Die with the Music in You

I was bumming around in Australia after I graduated. I was only there for a year and was hoping to stay on until my visa expired and hopefully find work in Australia in the process. I have always wanted to live in Australia since I was nine after reading about the country in Geography class and mesmerised with the stories of kangaroos and cows.

I remembered my father asking me to come home to Kuching to celebrate Lunar New Year that year but I said no because I had one more subject to finish and also, it would cost too much money. I could almost hear the desperation in his voice. At that time, I had gone down to Melbourne from Queensland to stay with my friend. I remember this so vividly.

My friends and I were all watching the opening ceremony of the Summer Olympics in Barcelona and then we all went to sleep. And then the dreaded early morning call from my cousin who also lived in Melbourne. She had received a call that my father had passed away. I was in a state of shock and could not even cry. A few hours later, I received another call to say that he had been resuscitated and was breathing again, though he was now in a comatose state.

And so began the longest journey home. I could not go back immediately because I had to sort out some things in Queensland. That took one day. I could not fly back to Kuching directly and had to transit in Singapore, which took another day before I could finally arrive in Kuching.

Fortunately, my father was still alive when I arrived. And so began a period of about three months when I had to take care of him. I learned to feed him through the tube. My mother would take the morning shift, my eldest brother the evening and me the night shift. We took the resuscitator off him after a few weeks because fortunately, he could breathe on his own. He never got out of the comatose state. It was September 30, two months short of his 60th birthday that he finally passed and I was the only one who saw him take his last breath.

Let me tell you about my father. His name is Liu Jam Hin. He was given the name Bob by English colleagues. He was born in Bau in Sarawak from a well-to-do family, the fourth son and sixth child. My grandfather and great-grandfather literally owned a gold mine. It all ended with the Second World War and his father died when he was 12. So unfortunately, he never got to enjoy the family's wealth.

When he was 17, he went over to Brunei and became a driller for Brunei Shell. He literally drilled for oil and was offshore every two weeks. It was a laborious and dangerous job. By the time I was born, he had already been promoted to a fairly senior position and did not have to go offshore anymore.

He was a loving father to his four children and a wonderful husband to my mother. It's not often you see Asian couples who are still in love 30 years into the marriage so they set the benchmark for a loving marriage. When I left from Kuching to Kuala Lumpur to further my studies (I'm still in the same country), we spent a whole night crying in each other's arms.

I think of people and their circumstances. My eldest uncle had the most education so he had the best opportunity also working for Shell in Brunei. My youngest uncle migrated to Canada and I have never met him. My second uncle sailed away from Borneo to New York to join a band (quite radical in the 1950s and 1960s). My father took the tried-and-trusted route because he also contributed to his mother's upkeep back home.

My father was a talented musician. He sounded like Nat King Cole and he could play instruments by ear. He could play the piano at home and before he got married, he was in a band playing the trumpet. I wonder how his life would have panned out if things were different.

For the Chinese, it's seen as good luck if you live through five 12-year cycles, but he didn't even make it that far. I wish he could have seen me reading the news. I wish I could have spoiled him and taken him on nice holidays and fancy meals. I wish he saw his grandson.

When I was still working at the hotel in my teens, I bought him a plush towel from the hotel. He used it until it was tattered and torn. I knew it meant the world to him. My only gift to him with my own money. I wonder how he would have lived the rest of his life without any major monetary concerns. Would he be willing to spend a little bit on himself on things he liked? Would he have pursued his music? In my eyes, he did everything as a father and more, with love, time and plenty of hugs.

I could go on and on about my father. All I can say is that I am blessed to have known him for 22 years of my life, although the last few months we didn't get to talk. Many times I still rewind back to the time I didn't see him during the Lunar New Year. What is done is done, I guess. Treasure the people you have with you while you can. Live life purposefully and meaningfully. Don't have regrets. Do things you want to do (Disclaimer: Don't hurt other people in the process).

Life Lesson: Live fully. Live meaningfully. Say the things you want to say to the people you care for.

Marriage: Cause and Effect

I met my ex-husband when I was 17. He was visiting the ice-cream parlour outside my school. He was there to meet my friend whom I thought he liked. I found out later it was a different story. Apparently he had seen me with this girl at another party and had asked his friend to invite me but the guy invited my friend instead. How juvenile, innocent and funny when you are 17.

We became penpals and would write letters to each other while he was studying in the UK. We met again in Singapore when I was 22 and love blossomed then. That was when the party mishap was revealed. We settled into a relationship and got married five years later. He was a good, dedicated and loving husband.

We were registered on October 31, Halloween. We took a trip to the UK and France before we "settled" down. Funny when you think about it: I remember being hesitant about marrying him but I thought people in general just had cold feet before getting married. We finally had a wedding ceremony four years later.

I have dedicated this part of the book to all the right things that happened because he was an important chapter in my life and also, I need to point out where I went wrong. He was always supportive of my endeavours. He had started his own business by then and I was the one with the stable job working for IBM, so I encouraged him to pursue his dreams.

One of the reasons why I married him was that early in our relationship, I got pregnant. I was not ready to settle then because I thought it would interrupt my career plans and we were not stable financially. He was totally opposed to an abortion and said it was not a case of saving face. He was angry with me for a year after I proceeded with the abortion but the fact that he chose to stand by me made me love him more.

I was paying for the mortgage and the medical bills, thanks to the job at IBM, while he would take care of the smaller bills. He started his business a month before the 1998 financial crisis in Asia so we had to laugh. There were no major bills then other than the home we bought together. He did develop hypertension at 28 though. I don't think it was because of me ...

Along the way, things changed for me that took away my attention: my job, having a child in my thirties and a business we started that made me edgy all the time. Sometimes we take for granted the people we are closest to. I still have flashbacks of moments where I treated him badly, nay, emasculated him, and he didn't fight back.

Suddenly the communication stopped. Holidays were always kept on hold. I stopped being loving, not even calling him when he went overseas. I stopped being intimate because I was just tired all the time. I have learned that doing that is a very dangerous thing.

I find it very difficult to write this part of the chapter and yet it is so necessary. I have always wondered whether I would be married so young if there were no biological clock. I have no regrets marrying him as it was a decision I made with my eyes wide open. Besides, I wouldn't have had my son. There were no societal pressures to get married but maybe they were self-imposed. You know the usual: meet someone in your twenties and get married and have your children in your twenties to thirties. Tick Tock, Tick Tock.

You will read in the later stages about my divorce. I am choosing to be a victor and not a victim in this situation. He does things that irk me now because I still have to communicate with him as the father of my child. That's a choice I have made, to make this arrangement as civil as possible.

I thank him for renovating the home we shared. I thank him for buying me gifts (which I thought was a waste of money). I thank him for being a gentleman and footing the household bills and the financial costs of my son. I know most men bail out so I am grateful. I thank him for making a large part of my life fairly carefree. I thank him for teaching me to appreciate the finer things in life and not be such a worry wart (this one is a tough one for me). In fact, he still buys meals for me and our son. He is a good son to his mother and that was one of the most attractive things about him. Among the three sons his mother had, he still bears the largest responsibility of taking care of her.

And so, I choose to operate at cause and not effect. In Neuro Linguistic Programming (NLP), we learn to understand where a person is not empowered and fail to see the relationship between their problem/issue/pattern and themselves. The idea is to see if you can get them back to cause to regain control.

Seeing the effect will mean that only he was wrong in the breakdown of the marriage. I cannot control him on his behaviour and being in this state will continue to disempower me. I would like to get back to cause where my behaviour had a role to play in the effect. That way, when I get back to cause and look at my own behaviour, I have the ability to control my own behaviour and learn from that experience. The idea is also not to repeat the mistakes I made. It takes two hands to clap.

Justified, there are some bad hats out there and try as you might, you cannot fathom where you are at fault. However, if you really think about it, there are ways to get back to cause. You will feel more empowered and optimistic in the process because you can control your own behaviour. So Bee, thanks for the memories.

Life Lesson: It's not rocket science but treat your life partner with respect and love. Communicate honestly and transparently.

People Skills

When I was working for IBM, a colleague approached me to join a network marketing business. It was very mysterious when he approached me and I was totally opposed to the idea of direct selling. It's funny how we have misconceptions about something even when we have no direct experience of it.

Seeing my father have his contract terminated three years earlier than expected always left me thinking about job security and the dependence on one source of income. And despite knowing that, we follow the same path because that's the only thing we know. Of course, I thought having a degree would make a difference. It's not really an advantage now, when everyone else also has a degree.

I had read the book *Rich Dad, Poor Dad* by Robert Kiyosaki and his subsequent book called *Cashflow Quadrant* and learned that we can earn income from one of four categories: being employed, self-employed, a business owner and an investor. This really put me on a trajectory of thinking about the many ways of earning income. Why earn income from one way when you can earn from multiple ways? Financial security is of ultimate importance to me. There are various ways of earning passive income. Some popular methods include fixed deposits, investments, rentals and royalties.

When I was working at my full-time job, I was already earning other sources of income. I was a part-time TV and radio newsreader. At one point I had three sources of income. I also tried my hand as a part-time lecturer. I asked myself: How long can I do this for? How long will I have the energy? When will I have the time for something else? When will I have time for children when I have them one day? Can I ever catch up in this hamster wheel of life? Yes, I like asking the tough questions. I don't want to be an ostrich with my head stuck in the sand.

When you are always trading time for money, something will give way. It could be your health or your relationships. It's ok when you're younger but what happens when you're older? One of my traits which I am very proud of is diligence. I am a hard worker. However, I also have to be clear with my end goal. The recent global pandemic resulted in businesses closing, jobs lost and at best, pay cuts. That is the unpredictability of life.

While keeping my job, my evenings were spent building a business that gave me passive income. It also opened my eyes to other avenues of passive income like property and investments. So I was looking at not only one source of passive income but multiple sources too. And if you can earn income from the four quadrants mentioned by Robert Kiyosaki, why not? Why limit yourself to only one quadrant?

Yet I still felt like I was searching for something but did not know what or how. Hence, I embarked on a journey in network marketing. In this business, I was taught to dream again and more importantly, to dream big. I was educated on duplicatable systems and why processes are important. I had continuous learning in the form of audio material, books and seminars. I learned how to work in teams.

In fact, my love for books was reignited because of this programme. Some insightful books include *The Magic Of Thinking Big*, where I learned we all have this disease called "excusitis"; *Personality Plus*, which helped me understand the pros and cons of my and other personalities and how to get to common ground; and *The Five Love Languages*, about how we have different languages in the form of acts of service, quality time, physical touch, gifts and words of affirmation. It made me understand people better.

I had access to wonderful products and a company that's the leading player in its field, having been around for close to 60 years. I still use the Amway products from their Nutrilite vitamins to Artistry skincare because they are effective.

What were the other life skills I learned from joining this business? I learned about leadership. When you have a team of volunteers and everyone is in business for themselves, you can't "instruct" people because they are not your employees. I learned about the intricacies of teamwork.

Listening skills was also an important lesson. I believe these skills help me today when I conduct interviews: to listen not just to affirm or defend but to discover other people's motivations. Another eye-opener for me was rejection. Not everyone is going to join the business and it's ok, I have to learn not to take it personally. People have different maps of the world and so they will see things differently.

A big one is humility. Like I said earlier, people have misconceptions about this business and think that people who do this are of a "certain" kind. I strongly believe in this business until today and so when people look at you suspiciously, you learn to swallow your pride and just take it as it comes. I absolutely enjoy how network marketing has enriched my life and led me to where I am today. I have become quite thick-skinned!

Although I am not actively building this business anymore, I still read the recommended books and attend the seminars. The seminars put me in an environment of positive people, keeps me humble, reminds me of how far I have come as a person plus how much I have to learn. I want to be in the company of big thinkers and stand on the shoulders of giants. Your income (and happiness) is the average of your five closest friends. If you don't like the average, expand your circle! What's crucial is the thinking and mindsets of the people you hang around with. We should use the understanding gained by major thinkers who have gone before in order to make intellectual progress. I don't know what I don't know and I don't pretend to know something from hearsay.

I still earn the passive income from this business. This is for the work I did ages ago and it's still paying me. It's not a huge amount but the returns have been consistent and regular. The other returns I feel are priceless. I have made some very genuine friends from building this business, people I do life with. So don't judge what you don't know until you've experienced it or are immersed in it. It's a bit like swimming. You can't learn to swim watching a video. The lessons beyond money have been invaluable.

Life Lesson: Look at sources of passive income. Be it fixed deposits or properties or anything in between. It's never too early or too late to start.

Stay Humble

How did I get into broadcasting? It was one of the most bizarre divine interventions in my life. I had no ambitions to go into this field at all. Growing up in Seria in Brunei where Shell was located, I used to listen to BFBS (British Forces Broadcasting Station), since Brunei at that time was still a British protectorate and the army was located there. I grew up listening to the UK's *Top of the Pops*. The station was so small that only our district received the AM transmission; even the capital city could not receive it. With not much choice of entertainment in Brunei generally, this was definitely one of the highlights growing up.

While I was taking care of my father in hospital, my sister's friend Suzie Chan asked if I would like to audition for Radio Televisyen Malaysia (RTM) Kuching. Now, Kuching is a small town so nothing major could be happening here. Obviously I turned her down because I was taking care of my father then.

Fast forward four or five months later, Suzie asked me the question again. By then my father had passed away and I was taking a break for about a month or so. I asked my mother's permission to check it out because I wasn't doing anything anyway.

So I met with the producer (I think) and we just started talking. If it was an audition, I wasn't aware at all but I received a call that I got the part. A part of what, I still didn't know. I thought it would be a local variety show of sorts. It would be a good experience, I thought to myself. I was thinking hard then about my future career plans in either public relations or advertising.

I was then called and given the brief for the show. OMG! It was a live telecast aired over Singapore, Brunei and Malaysia. Every two years, a variety show was held in either Singapore or Malaysia (wherever there is an RTM station). That year, it happened to be in Kuching. They had a male host who spoke in

Bahasa Malaysia and they were looking for a female host who had to be Sarawakian and could speak English.

During rehearsals, I had the chance to meet these big stars from Singapore and Malaysia. It was the first time I was on TV, and it was live! It so happened that the heads of Singapore Broadcasting Corporation (SBC, now known as MediaCorp) and of course RTM were there and saw me. They must have seen something in me.

I was asked by SBC to host their Countdown show in Singapore for New Year's a month later and this was where I was reunited with my future husband who was working there at the time. This was another live show and by this time, I was almost ready. It was a baptism of fire indeed. While I was there, they asked me to apply for a job which I did not get. I wasn't keen though because I still didn't think there was a future in broadcasting. If I had wanted a career in broadcasting then, it would either be Hong Kong or the US.

Meanwhile, when I headed back to Kuching, I was also asked by RTM to join them full-time and actually to host Selamat Pagi Malaysia (RTM's morning show) in Bahasa Malaysia which I declined because I wasn't fluent in it. A lesson here is to recognise what is not a core strength!

RTM also organised a private audition for me (how blessed I am!) and I got a message that if I ever decided to go to Kuala Lumpur, I would have a job there reading the news. I was thankful but still determined not to do this full-time. I finally got a job in a PR consultancy in Kuala Lumpur in June the following year and got settled in after a few months.

And after a few months getting accustomed to my day job, I informed the late Mohd Salled Pateh Akhir (Deputy Director-

General) that I was ready to come on air as a part-timer. Along came the practice sessions and that's how the story goes. The whole journey took almost a year but I was not in a hurry.

Another person I should mention is George Abraham who headed Radio 4 in RTM (now TraXX FM) and he invited me to present on radio as well. I would get calls from him at the end of each read

Reading the news on national TV in the 1990s. No, it was not North Korean TV!

where he would correct me on my pronunciation and diction. I absolutely loved it because he came from a place of love and kindness. When you don't have visuals to hide your flaws, radio taught me more about speaking well. So I ended up reading news on both radio and TV for more than 15 years. I also hosted a few morning shows as well.

One thing I took from all this was to remain humble. Be firm with your beliefs and values. When you decide to do something, do it wholeheartedly and to the best of your ability. Always be willing to learn and always act like a rookie with a lot more to learn. I definitely do because there really is a lot I still don't know. Even to this day, I listen to native English speakers on certain words which I have mispronounced over the years.

Serendipity? If my father was not ill, I would not be back from Australia then. Everything happens for a reason. During this period, I was never caught up in the glamour of being on

TV. There were opportunities to schmooze but I was totally not interested. I was in it for the side income and the lessons it taught me: to be able to learn a craft and to master it.

I never take these opportunities for granted and if it wasn't for the people who believed in me during my early days, I wouldn't have gotten to where I was when it came to presenting a show. In fact, broadcasting has been the most consistent thing in my life, and I have been doing this for almost 30 years. Wow, to say this out loud. To think I never wanted to do this full-time too!

Life Lesson: Always have a mindset of a rookie with a willingness to learn because you always will have something to learn.

Know Your Values

Looking back, I have never had just one job at any one time. I was born to be a hustler with side gigs. There are now terminologies for this kind of behaviour so I'm not abnormal! When I was working as a receptionist at Kuching Hilton, I was also a choral singer. When I started my work in a PR consultancy (thanks Shah Ghani for hiring me) and subsequently at IBM, I was a part-time newsreader, network marketer, lecturer and emcee. Even now, at this stage in my life, I am writing books and doing emcee work.

This could be mental conditioning watching my father not have his contract renewed. I've learned not to depend on one job for security. Having read Robert Kiyosaki's books like *Rich Dad, Poor Dad* and *Cashflow Quadrant*, it is a fact that there is no such thing as job security and that's just the way the cookie crumbles.

In deciding on your career, work or life, it's so important to stick to your values. I didn't fully comprehend it then. I am really fortunate to have worked with companies which were flexible; maybe I purposely looked for them or maybe I made them flexible.

When I got the job as a part-time news presenter on RTM, I remember just marching in to my boss's office and informing her of it, not even asking. I seriously thought that as a PR consultancy, they would benefit from having someone in their office working in media as well. The point here is that if we believe in certain values, we should have the courage of our convictions.

This realisation of my values and what is important to me came about when I was in the midst of leaving the consultancy and looking for a job on the client side of things. Obviously I wanted to work for a multinational company. I had two job interviews at that time: IBM (my preferred choice because it was close to home) and a prominent American bank.

The interview process for both these companies was long. At the end, both of them offered me a role. Picture this. The bank was offering almost twice my previous pay plus all the other banking perks. At this stage in my life, I was planning to buy a home and the discounted loans would come in very, very handy.

IBM offered marginally lesser but it was much closer to home and technology seemed like an interesting area to go into. It didn't have as many benefits as the bank but they were fairly good as well. Do you know what was the determining factor in my decision? Never, ever let it be money, as appealing as that is.

Let me tell you what happened. Before signing on the dotted line, I asked the bank if my working as a part-time news presenter was an issue. They said yes it was, even though I only worked weekends and during the evenings and the day job would always be my priority. The interviewing manager said, "People will know you work for this bank and think we don't pay you enough."

I asked IBM the same question and their answer was, "No problem!" Mind you, I wasn't exactly being paid a lot by the TV or radio station, but that was not the point. What I valued were flexibility, openness and opportunities for growth. And it was difficult to hide the fact that I had a part-time job if I came out on TV and radio!

I felt the bank owned my life and soul even before signing on the dotted line. What more after I did! The decision was very clear then. It was to join IBM. Thank goodness I did. I stayed there for 11 years and it turned out to be a family-oriented company. Had I just looked at money, my judgement would have been clouded.

A recent visit to the company that gave me the chance to find my values and what mattered most to me.

I always ask people to be clear about why they want to join a company. If it's money and I fully understand that this is important, so be it. However, dig deeper to see how it's aligned back to your values and you will have more clarity on your decisions, not just in work but in your life.

For example, if I ever join another organisation, the money will be a factor but not the most important factor. My more important questions will be: How flexible are the working conditions and will I have the freedom to pursue other non-competitive projects? Will there be opportunities for growth? Will I be learning new skills in new industries?

I took a 30% pay cut from IBM to join BFM because it was an industry I wanted to join. There has never been a business radio station which was talk radio, a format I have never tried. It was an opportunity for *kaizen*, a Japanese term for "continuous improvement". If it didn't work out, I could always go back to public relations.

I am not sharing this story from a position of privilege. It was hard work and dedication. When I came to KL, I paid for my own expenses, that is, no one paid rent for me. I rented a room which was affordable. I didn't get a car until two years later. I put the down payment to my first Kancil from my own blood, sweat and tears. And so it was a case of developing survival and adaptable skills. It's important to reskill, upskill and to continue being relevant to the times. Technology is changing the way the world operates and so we must adapt.

Another reason why flexibility is important. I am still eternally grateful to this day that IBM offered me a two-year sabbatical while I worked at BFM. In this period, they continued to pay for my medical and dental expenses. If all failed at BFM, I could still go back to IBM. See what happens when you join an organisation that connects with your values?

Life Lesson: Find out what matters to you. Really. Not what popular rhetoric tells you. Once you've elicited these values, it's easier to make decisions.

Money, Money, Money

I have covered this in almost every story from my twenties. This is important and I believe a whole chapter needs to be dedicated to this topic. A lot of people, especially women, don't like talking about money or fancy discussing the intricacies of money. I personally don't like it either.

Let me tell you about my father. If you have been through a death in the family, the paperwork is complicated. This is my father without much to his name but he always thought things through. He had one file for the car, one file for the house and files for properties shared with my mother. The files were in the cupboard and upon his death, there was no need for a great search for them.

Even with all this simplicity, it was not smooth running. I also watched my mother having to handle things. She had the kids to help her out but still, there was a sense of hopelessness because she had just lost the love of her life. Being level-headed while heartbroken is not easy.

That probably got me on a journey of being wary of finances. Yes, my eyes still glaze over when people start going into figures and using jargon. So get educated and look around for people who can talk to you about money in a simplistic manner. I know I did. Sometimes they talk until they tire me out and I just sign on the dotted line. I am only kidding.

First things first, buy insurance the moment you start working. I did not have much money then. I was paying rental for a room, payment for my car and I bought insurance. If anything should happen to me, my mother would be burdened to take care of me. She's already elderly and the last thing she needs was for me to be a financial burden. So yes, it might be a stretch in the beginning but it gets easier the older you get.

As you get older and your life changes, look at ways of topping up the insurance. I bought an education insurance for my son and if he doesn't need it to pay for his education, then I can pass on this insurance policy to him. God forbid, should he fall ill earlier (or later), he has some protection.

I also bought insurance for a medical card. The hospitalisation bills will deplete you. If you are faced with a major illness, the last thing you want to think about is finances. I have a friend who had breast cancer and used up all her insurance money. She could not get a permanent job after that because of her medical history. She was separated from her husband and he wasn't able to provide financially. She had two young daughters and if it wasn't for their single aunt, the situation would have been worse. Once you have bought the insurance and claimed it, you will not be able to buy another insurance policy. Harsh but true.

This was when I was working for IBM, which provided excellent coverage. Company insurance is great if you are working there. But life changes and you may not work for that organisation forever so you better be prepared should the situation change. Be like a Boy Scout and "Be Prepared".

I got my first credit card six months after I started work. You feel so grown up getting one. And then you will be tempted to go wild. Of course I went insane the first few months and when you realise you've resorted to paying the minimum amount due, you know you're in serious trouble and about to go down that rabbit hole. It probably took me about six months to sort out that amount. The interest keeps going up and it gets more challenging to cover the hole you've dug. Moral of the story is not to spend more than you can afford. Sounds so simple, right? But many people get lulled into the trap. To this day, if I cannot afford to pay the full amount next month, then I know I have overspent!

The fancy holidays can wait for a while. This was life before low-cost flights and holidays being more accessible so yes, these were the things I had to forego temporarily. Forget the frills for now because the rewards will come. I would rather "suffer" now then pay for the consequences later.

On to my last financial consideration. I wrote my will in my thirties. Yes, we can't escape two things in life: death and taxes. Of course if you're working in Dubai or Brunei, you can still escape taxes. Basically the moment you have properties or possessions, you should be looking at getting a will. In my case, it was the properties and the birth of my son.

I was married then and I was reliving what my mother went through. I knew the importance of a will. Don't let history repeat itself. Every experience can be a learning intersection for us if we let it. When other lives are involved, try to make it as simple as possible for them when the untimely does happen. Later, when I got divorced, I relooked at my finances again, from insurance and my will to who gets my money in the Employee Provident Fund.

For me, sorting all these icky things meant my mind was clear to do more productive things. We all have these niggling thoughts on unfinished business and it's hard to focus on anything productive if something is holding you back. The mind is not a storage cabinet. When there's peace of mind, you can get into the zone and the flow to do the things you enjoy. Things that trouble you mentally will affect everything you do and worse still, may even manifest in your health.

Evaluate your finances every 10 years or so or when life changes. We are all inevitably getting older and so it is important to sort it out for your own life and people who have to take care of you.

Life Lesson: When you fail to plan, you plan to fail. Understand how to manage your personal finances.

STAGE 4

THE COCOONED YEARS

I have pretty much lived my life as textbooks dictated at this stage. I was fairly entrenched in my day job at IBM and my TV and radio news presenting plus my network marketing business. Everything was going as planned. Sometimes I wonder if they're my plans or plans expected by society. No one really puts a gun to your head.

Having a baby does change you though. You don't live for yourself anymore. This helpless being who didn't ask to be born and was brought into this world. You will do everything in your ability to protect and nurture your child. Something definitely changes. Priorities do.

One thing I was glad I did was that I never forgot myself. As much as I love my son, he is my world but he's not the only thing. I know that one day I have to live out the rest of my life and I really have to get used to being my own person. None of us are one-dimensional. I am a mother, daughter, employee, daughter-in-law, news presenter, colleague, network builder and the list goes on.

I talked a lot about the Wheel of Life in my previous book and that is how I live nowadays. One thing I should have done a lot more when I had a new baby was nurture the relationship with my ex-husband. Things take on different priorities each year and as seasons change but no area in the Wheel of Life should be ignored.

The Wheel of Life comes up to eight or ten components but let me list out the eight: finance, family, friends, community, fun, fitness, faith and career. This could be extended to include mental growth and relationships. Make sure you have goals in all these areas and it could be something as simple as reading 15 minutes a day for mental growth to finishing a marathon for fitness. Only you can dictate what's important to you.

Now that you have heard of the Wheel of Life, regardless of your age, start working out some goals in all areas of the Wheel of Life. Review this yearly and once you've made a decision on some goal, stick at it for a year. If something needs to be improved, some change de-prioritised, do it next year.

I once organised a retreat and someone said they were at zero when it came to faith and I said faith does not mean a religion, it could be some sort of spirituality. Really, to me, it's about an anchor when times are tough: to figure out what's your anchor and to strengthen that anchor.

Doing a session with Supparetreat in 2019. Events like these make me realise I do enjoy training, coaching and facilitating.

Oh yes, take care of your health. If you haven't started making changes for your health, better start now. Suddenly, the metabolic rate isn't so high anymore. It sure is much harder to lose weight too.

The almost-10 years of being able to watch my son grow and be with him can never be returned. I was blessed to have a job that allowed me to work and be a stay-at-home mother too. I was working from home as I had a regional role and so I was location-agnostic. This was a path I chose to take when I decided to join IBM which I knew gave me that option. Had I joined the bank, I am not sure if this option would be available. There are no bad choices but we make them right.

Even if you can afford it and can choose not to work to raise kids, keep a pulse of what's happening in the job market. Financial independence is so vital to me. Look at ways to earn sources of income. It may not be much but at least it gives you a sense of control.

A lot of women face challenges when going back to work. I feel it is the lack of confidence rather than skills. And even if you don't have skills, there are plenty of places to learn these skills. They may seem trivial but they're not. Future employers would appreciate that you are resourceful and have kept up-to-date with the changes in the marketplace.

It's called preparation meets opportunity. If you seriously have the luxury of not needing to work for money, your skills will also come in handy should you choose to help out in community causes. Yes, find an interest outside of home. It makes for a better relationship with your spouse and children down the road.

We know stories of meddling parents when the child is single, married and even after having children. That usually happens when their children are their whole world. I really don't want to end up being that meddling mother or mother-in-law.

A lot of women in their thirties are also choosing to build their careers during this period. Don't have career-envy if that is not your path. It's when we start making comparisons, that's when we get dissatisfied. My career at that point was not my top priority and that was the decision I chose to make at that point. It looked like I was cocooned career-wise, but really I was focusing on my young family. Like a caterpillar which looks like it is resting, I was still growing on the inside.

Whenever I make a major life decision, I normally don't just think of the present moment, I do have a view of what things are going to be like five or ten years down the road. If I didn't spend time with my son during his early years, five to ten years down we won't have much of a relationship. I know I will be wracked with guilt too. As he's a teenager now and avoiding me at all costs, I am not sure it's enough!

As important as my son is, know that we're all multi-faceted people. You could be a mother, aunt, sister, daughter-in-law, employer, employee, investor, daughter, caregiver, manager ... well, you get what I mean. Some roles can be all-encompassing at certain stages of life and once we've committed to that, it's all temporary until we get to another stage in life.

Here are some questions you can ask yourself. What gives you energy? What excited you when you woke up today? What is the most fearless thing you did today? Tomorrow? What negative thoughts hold you back? What positive thoughts help you move forward? How do you cultivate those positive thoughts?

How have you grown this week? What did you learn? Did you enjoy the work you did today? How do you move closer to your dream job this week? What could you be happy about if you chose to be? What will give you inner peace? What are you passionate about?

What will your legacy be one day? How can you start working on that this week? What's the biggest goal you want to achieve over the next year? What can you do this week to get started? What are you most proud of in your life? Did you make yourself proud today? What is the biggest change you're willing to make this week?

What would you do if you knew you couldn't fail? How would your life change if you acted in faith vs in fear? If you were to fully live your life, what is the first change you'd make? What's missing in your life right now? Where does your life need the biggest upgrade?

What needs to shift in order to live your dream life? How can you focus on that shift tomorrow? Next month? What three habits do you have that don't support or uplift you? What do you need to do to replace them? What are you still holding on to? How does it benefit you to hold on? How will it benefit if you let go?

Imagine for a moment you're living your dream life, what are you saying to yourself? What do others notice about you? How does it feel? This barrage of questions takes time to fill. Get deep with yourself and do a due diligence or audit on your life. Have an immediate view of your life but do take a look for the mid-term and the long-term too. When the empty nest hits, you will be faced with a loss or sense of purpose because you didn't prepare for the future.

And Then Came Baby

Jude was conceived on the day of my wedding, not to be confused with the day I signed the marriage papers, which was four years earlier. He was born at 40 weeks and 5 days at 3.6kg. Yes, he was late. It was one of the happiest days of my life.

I did not suffer from any morning sickness. I did not have any cravings. I basically ate everything. I generally do not like the cold but with him, I felt hot all the time. I could eat half a melon every day just to cool down which could explain the excessive weight I put on.

Truth be told, I was not planning on having a child just yet. So when I found out I was pregnant, I was actually upset because this wasn't part of the "plan". I was already in my thirties though. I started crying at the gynaecologist. I now realise that my tears were the realisation that I was now responsible for another life.

Once I came to acceptance (very quickly), I embraced the pregnancy in all its glory. Both mother and son were huge. Fortunately I didn't have complications like hypertension or diabetes. I think from the third trimester, I didn't feel any movement. The only way I found out how he was every day was dropping the toilet seat which emitted a loud noise. That way I got a slight kick from him.

After waiting for him to come out for five days, my water finally broke. Fortunately, it was a public holiday in Selangor and morning traffic was fine. The water bag broke at 7am and I didn't dilate. By 7pm, the doctor said the baby was stressed and so I had to opt for a C-section.

Something takes over the moment you become a mother. You become a mama bear and would do anything to protect your baby. Of course, hormones are in full gear after delivery. I understand how people can become depressed without help. I solicited the help of my mother, mother-in-law and a domestic helper to protect this bundle of joy and yet, it sometimes still felt insufficient.

One of the best decisions I made was working for IBM. There were very few companies then (and even now) which offered the work-from-home option. I took on a regional job which allowed me to work from home. This I did for six years until he went to Primary 1. Even though I didn't have to look into the minute needs like cooking and cleaning, I wanted to be there for him when he came back from kindy. It's the joy of seeing him, smelling him and reading bedtime stories.

A mentor of mine, Basil Harris, once mentioned to me: "Do not deny your children the privilege of struggle." I believe my parents gave me that gift unwittingly! Although I resented it when my parents didn't have the funds for an overseas education, my forced resourcefulness made me resourceful in life (see story in Stage 2). Obstacles can be overcome: around it, through it, over it and under it.

Another wise saying is "Children are temporary guests in our household." That one got me thinking a lot. Really children never "belong" to us. They are under our care but we don't own them. What does it mean to me? If they are temporary guests, you treat them well with care and love and know one day they will leave to live their own lives.

I will do my part to be the best mother but I also have to be prepared that he won't be tied to my apron strings for the rest of his life. He has to forge on in his own life, be independent and do what he needs to do without his mother emotionally blackmailing him. Emotional blackmailing will only hinder his progress mentally.

It also means that I have to be independent and live my own life with him, secure in the knowledge that his mother will be fine, loves him immensely and unconditionally and will be there for him ... in the background. And so, I live independently at this point in my life as my son is getting ready to spread his wings.

Be it sons to mothers (Mama's boy) or daughters to fathers (Daddy's girl), let your children go. A measure of my success as a mother is that he grows up to be a man who honours me and is able to fend for himself without his parents bailing him out when he gets into trouble (hopefully never).

Parents, don't guilt-trip your children. Have honest conversations if you have something on your mind. I am glad I spent his early days with him and "eased" myself from him in his teenage years. As I am writing this, he is almost 18 and hates it when his mother treats him like a baby (old habits die hard) but he knows I do in jest. I'd rather he be honest with his thoughts and feelings than keep things away from me.

When I am wrong, I apologise. He needs to know that as a parent I do make mistakes and I also know how to say I am sorry. These are the qualities I want him to have. I will always be a parent to him and not a friend whom he feels he can disrespect. Sometimes, I have flashbacks of what I was like to my mother and he's a gem in comparison.

I have always wanted another child but to me that meant more time and financial commitment. The time commitment would have been a bigger factor. The father of my child had never been very participatory in raising him, be it taking him to the park or sending him to classes and things like that. That's the way he is from watching how his father behaved. If I had another child, it would mean being concerned for his upbringing right down to his education and the yoke would be heavier on my part. I am not willing to sacrifice the mental commitment for another child.

And I think this is an important factor beyond money. The important question you have to ask yourself is if you are prepared to do this for the long haul. The answer to that can only be given truthfully by yourself and to yourself. I know my ex-husband was not geared to be paternal in nature. I am not that maternal either. So only if I can physically and mentally be committed and prepared, will I have another child. Otherwise you will go through unnecessary anguish and stress by having more children because society expects you too.

I definitely haven't worked out parenting and yes, like most parents, I often second guess myself. That's why I am not afraid to apologise to my son. I always wonder if I had spent more time reading to him, he would enjoy reading more ... plus many other concerns. Ask me in 10 years' time if my strategy worked!

Life Lesson: Treat your children well and treat them right. They are not going to stay forever and don't pressure them to. Our children have their own journey to make.

Have an Anchor in Life

So at that point, life was going smoothly fairly. My husband at that time was getting more established in his business. We had bought another home to accommodate the expanding family: a new baby, one of our mothers (mine or his would with stay us every three months on a rotational basis from Kuching) and a live-in helper.

All throughout my life, I have always believed in Jesus Christ. I never had to go searching for which god was the right one. Many times He came knocking on my door but I would not open it because I always felt unworthy and guilty of many sins. I think I must have been nine years old when this preacher came to my school and that was when I felt God's love. I was not brought up in a Christian household although my father accepted Christ in his life a year before he died.

A few years into my ex-husband's business, his partner decided to go separate ways. Things changed when more money came in and when he hired his wife into the business. I have never liked that guy but my ex had always been defensive of his friends.

Another whammy we were dealt with was that his partner never changed the business to a partnership and kept it as a sole proprietorship. He had thought he was partners with his friend. As a chartered quantity surveyor, that meant all his work for the last five years would not be recognised as his and he had to start again.

So what could we do? He wrote to the Institute of Surveyors Malaysia (ISM) and decided to try his luck on something that had never been done. He requested for a split partnership so that his past recognitions would be recognised. I could only be a reassuring wife at that point and say I would stand by him no matter what. We were not young but not exactly old, and so we could begin again. We were faced with the investments we'd made like the new house and a new baby, but decided to take it one day at a time. Strangely, I was not too worried. And so we waited for the results. We had gone back to Kuching for Chinese New Year though I knew he was not in the mood to celebrate.

It was the eve of Chinese New Year and he received a call at lunchtime. I was sitting next to him and ISM told him his request for his new business was approved. He was overjoyed and at that moment I said, "That was God. We have to go to church." He had to agree it was God because it was indeed supernatural.

The number of times the supernatural has happened to me are countless.

The moment we went back to Kuala Lumpur, we went church hunting. We visited a few churches and we finally settled on one where we felt both at home. I was willing to go to whichever he felt comfortable in. It was also a time for my son at almost three years old to know who God was. I tell my son now that he's more grown up that the decision to follow God is his own, just like how it was for me.

However, it was quite a practical and methodical decision to go to church. I would attend what we would call a cell night when we met with fellow believers on a weekly basis in addition to weekly church attendance. I chose a home that was closest to mine and this is what we call a spiritual family. No, it wasn't perfect but tell me which family is! This family would come to my help at a later stage in my life and make me so glad I had invested in my spiritual life.

I talk about this in my last book, *In Your Skin*, about the importance of looking into the spiritual aspect of your life. Whatever you consider to be a spiritual anchor is totally up to you. It could be a song that you listen to or meditation. For me, it's been Jesus Christ. I am reminded of not who I am but whose I am.

When everything is stripped away from my identity, can I still stand strong and tall? My faith allows me to be authentic. I come with flaws and it's because I am flawed, I need my God. I have been told a few times not to talk too boldly about my faith but if I am afraid to acknowledge who is my Lord and Saviour, one day when I am knocking on heaven's door, maybe He won't acknowledge me either.

The danger of having a person as an anchor is that people will fail you. Of course, we have friends, relatives and spouses to count on but when your life is dependent on people in general, be prepared to be disappointed. Such is life and when you recognise that, you're mentally prepared.

My friend who has gone through two marriages and just ended a relationship is now on the hunt for another relationship. I have seen the tears in the last three years. It's like putting on a coat of paint on a wall that's not dry from the first layer. It looks like new but then the cracks will form in due time.

It's not that I don't trust people. In fact, I have a saying shared by a mentor: "Put a 10 on everyone's forehead" which means to treat people like a 10. Life is never black or white and always a bit grey. So it was during this life stage that I finally opened the door when He knocked. This was probably the season to be still, rest in Him and know that He's in charge if I fully depend on Him.

Life Lesson: Find your anchor. When the storms come (and they will), what will keep you steadfast?

Support Structure

During interviews, I always get asked how I balance my work and life and how I manage to juggle it all. I'm also always asked about the struggles I have gone through. Just think for a while. Do men get asked these questions? Are the words "juggle", "struggle" and "sacrifice" – just to name a few – used for men? After all, there are obstacles and challenges that every human goes through.

What is worrying though is that these questions are usually asked by women to women. Words have such an impact on our psyche. I don't use these words in my vocabulary. When I do use the word struggle it is probably when I am homeless and starving. I hope I never have to use the word.

Why am I talking about this? Women in general, and more so in Asia, have a Martha Complex. I thought I just made this up but it really is a term referring to extreme busyness. We actually get a kick out of the ability to "do it all". The root of this is the need for validation. And the result is pure exhaustion and possibly resentment.

If you are married, have a serious conversation with your spouse and children (those that are old enough) to share with household chores if you don't have the privilege of help with a cleaner. We have to change the status quo of things if we want things to change. Teach your children (boys and girls) that it's equal responsibility. Don't segregate what boys and girls can do. The education of gender equality begins at home.

If you are a single mother and you can afford it, do outsource help. Leaving these tasks to the experts meant I could make the best use of my time, and tap on my core strengths. When I had a kid, I had the help of my mother, mother-in-law and a domestic helper to assist in the running of the household and the care of my son. When I became a single mother, my mother-in-law continued living with me to provide as much normalcy as possible for my son. When my son got older and was at a school-going age, I solicited other assistance. For example, I arranged for transport to and from school. That way, I am not stressed in traffic. I had to pick him up from school a few times and as we were caught up in traffic, he was dead asleep in the car. It wasn't quality time because we didn't have a conversation and I was stressed.

Jude with both his grandmas on our annual holiday in 2015. Once the holiday ends, only memories remain. Both grandmas don't have the energy to travel now.

When I stopped having a live-in helper, I sought out the help of a trusted cleaner from the office who came by a few times a week; she had access to my house with her own set of keys. Of course, I trusted her completely so I could move freely to do other things and not watch her like a hawk. Dinner was catered and all we had to do was cook rice. If my son needed extra tuition, I got tutors who came to the house.

Be solution-oriented and if money can solve a problem so that your time could be spent doing something more productive, please do so. The time saved was spent thinking about ideas to build my brand, write more books and doing other creative pursuits. Don't beat yourself up if you are not geared in a certain way. We are all called to do different things and made differently.

I am truly blessed that my parents never made any stereotypical references when I was growing up as to what a boy or a girl should do. If they did, I probably wouldn't listen. A lot of it also comes from reading and being exposed to what is happening around the world. Take a leaf from the Scandinavians: in their part of the world, parental leave is almost equal between mothers and fathers. The current ambassador of Sweden in Malaysia is currently taking care of his two teenage daughters in Malaysia while his wife continues to build her career back in Sweden. What is so outstanding for me is so mainstream for them.

Know your stress buttons and find out how you can ease that. As I am writing this, we are in the midst of the Movement Control Order (Malaysia's term for lockdown) due to the coronavirus. My son and I are taking turns to sweep the porch and perform the basic household duties to keep the house clean. Now that's a struggle. I am only kidding. I have no time to cook because I am still working but thank goodness for food deliveries, I am less stressed.

Thank goodness for the people like my mother and my mother-in-law who have come to Kuala Lumpur to help me. I know it's a huge sacrifice for them too as they leave their hometowns to be here for their grandson. They would not have come here if I had not asked.

Don't be afraid to seek help if it helps to keep you sane. There is no loss in pride or face if you can't be at your best. Sit down and list the things that you have to do to manage the household or your life. Look at what is necessary, what you can do and what can possibly be outsourced. From what can be outsourced, can you get someone else to do it or simplify the process?

Now, I am living alone with my son. He knows how to cook when he wants to. I don't spend the weekends grocery shopping. I even get these delivered if I can. I may go out to buy fruits occasionally. Too much is spent prepping, cooking and cleaning for meals. And since there are only two of us, a lot of food is actually wasted. Now if you genuinely find pleasure in cooking, then that's a different story.

My point is to seek help whenever you can. There's no shame in not being able to do it all. We are all interdependent. You want to get a point of effectiveness and not fatigue. When there's clarity in thought and body, that's when you can move forward productively.

Life Lesson: Don't be a martyr when it comes to your life. Outsource non-essential services wherever you can.

Reskilling and Upskilling

I did get a bit bored during the cocooned years. People who know me know I cannot sit still figuratively and literally, hence my search for courses to attend. One of the courses I attended was called Money & You, which took a lot of its teachings from Buckminster Fuller. It basically addressed our individual attitudes towards money.

For example, if we think all rich people are crooks, guess what? We will have an issue being rich because of this belief. This bit of experiential learning was truly eye-opening. Seeing the difference between thinking of the world as abundant and the world as scarce really hit home. When we believe in an abundant world, you believe there are plenty of opportunities for all. It's a much better place to be in because you start thinking collaboratively and how it can be win-win for everyone.

I had heard of coaching by then and while on a long car ride from Johore back to Kuala Lumpur, I decided to embark on a course that provided coaching certification with the International Coaching Federation. As I was still working for IBM then, who contributed to the Human Resources Development Fund, I could actually redeem the course. My supervisor was quite smart and fair though, and made me pay for 50% of the course while the company paid for the other half.

This course opened my eyes to the importance of asking questions. The right kinds of questions. When posed with a difficult question, asking yourself why this has happened to you isn't exactly going to help you solve the problem. Instead, asking yourself how you can possibly resolve this situation gets you into solution mode. I learned to self-coach by asking the right questions.

Even then, sometimes we can be caught in a situation with our blinkers on and that's when you need to solicit help from outside, like another coach who can help you gain a new perspective. During the time I was taking the course, I had doubts on whether I should make a career move. Together with my course mates, I coached myself into taking the new job.

I then did both Practitioner and Master courses in Neuro Linguistic Programming or NLP. It was a great understanding of how the mind works. Sometimes it's already things we know but now we know what we know and we also know what we don't know. Here are some of the things it taught me. There is a concept called the map of the world and we all have different maps of the world. Where we are born, how we are educated, our faith, our experiences and our upbringing shape our views of the world.

Sometimes when we have a misunderstanding with a person, it's because their map of the world is different from ours. When we come into communication with anyone, it's good to come with the understanding that that's why we're different. It makes it all the more exciting that people can give us different perspectives and open our eyes to different worlds.

Congruence is another effective tool that helps in understanding how the mind works. When your actions and words don't match, you will feel an unease. You may be able to fool some people for a while and even yourself, but sooner or later, it'll get to you. When people talk about being authentic, that's what it means.

Another tool that we can use to see things clearly is the theatre concept. When we're too close to a situation, we can't see it. I use this tool to disassociate myself and watch the scene as a third-party and yes, sometimes when we watch the situation, I'll notice where I went wrong in the way I behaved and the words I used.

Rapport has been such a crucial tool I have learned to use. I learned developing rapport when I was actively building my network marketing business but learning the mechanics behind this has helped me as a communicator in radio and when I do moderating or emcee work. For example, I've learned to mirror someone to connect with them whether in our behaviour or by using similar words, so that we come to a point of agreement. Before I start my interviews, I take this time to put the person at ease so by the time they come on air, they feel like they are with a friend and can speak more comfortably.

I try to make a person laugh at least once if I can too. I always say that thousands have lost their radio virginity to me.

The moment two people laugh together, they've mirrored each other, and they automatically relax a bit more. It helps to be self-deprecating and human and it's just a much better world when we see each other as equals. It makes for better radio at the end of the day than a tongue-tied and nervous person! So, it's not rocket science but it's an art and a science to understand how the mind works.

I am currently doing a Post Graduate Diploma in Design Thinking. Why? I want to know the process of creativity and innovation and see if there are methods to them. With the future in the direction of artificial intelligence, machine learning and all this talk of Industry 4.0, what's going to make us stand apart? In fact, the principles of Design Thinking can be implemented into our lives as well.

I took up this online course before the Movement Control Order in Malaysia and I'm so glad I did. I am making the most of this situation by doing other online courses from Masterclass, LinkedIn Learning and other sources to get educated and ready for the new normal. The pandemic brought with it stories of businesses shut, job losses and pay cuts. Maybe you're salvaged from the situation now. Who is to say something of this sort won't happen again? Are you ready and prepared the next time around? My friend lost her job prior to the pandemic and now she's looking for another job in an already soft market. She's also older and getting a job is not as easy. That's a harsh reality of life.

I am also currently enrolled in a Journal Therapy course. Why? Journaling has helped me as an individual and if there's a process which I can do better, why not? Also, it's a tool I hope to be able to share with my coaching clients.

So far, I have been through three financial crises and recessions and now this pandemic. It's a VUCA (Volatile Uncertain Complex Ambiguous) world and the only thing we can do is simplify it. You can't stay cocooned or stick your head in the sand. So always be learning, always be growing. You don't know what you don't know. Isn't that exciting?

Life Lesson: Invest in yourself and keep reskilling and upskilling. The old ways have gone and it's the new normal.

BFM: Because Freda Matters

I had been working with IBM for 10 years by then. I started my career in the Communications team and became the PR manager for Malaysia the year after. In the 10 years I was there, I learned so much. I had the privilege to take on six different roles while I was there. First there was the regional role for ASEAN/India for the Enterprise Server Group and then for the Asia Pacific region handling the Financial Services Sector.

I took on a global project which was exciting and tiring at the same time. This was a global hiring tool called Global Opportunity Marketplace which was being launched in India and I was involved in the communication of this project. In the lead up to the launch, I was based in Bangalore for three weeks. I would wake up at 7am and head to the office, getting caught in traffic on the way. Upon arrival I would be attending calls with the rest of ASEAN (which was two hours ahead of us), even as I was taking care of India. In the afternoon, Europe would wake up and I would be involved in those calls too. Just when I thought I could go home, the US woke up and by the time I got back to the hotel after going through traffic again, it would be 9pm. Rinse and repeat.

I came back with vertigo. Lying down on my bed one day, the room started spinning. The doctor said it wasn't stress related but I am sure it was. It slowly disappeared and I am just glad that it's never returned since. Since the experience in India, which was the largest hiring country at that time, every other place has been much easier. I had to forego a free incentive trip to Italy because of this job. This role had me travelling to India, Shanghai and the UK, so it was very exciting.

Well, the project went for a year and a half and when it ended, there were no other roles in Communications at that time so I went into Marketing for Business Partners. It was hardly a marketing role. I was spending more time working out the processes and ensuring everyone got paid instead of doing any marketing. Soon, I was looking for a way out.

It was around that time that I got a call from an old friend, Noelle Lim, who told me there was a new independent business station that adopted the talk-show format and style. The first thing I asked was location because I wasn't willing to travel too far! Well, it was only a kilometre away and so I met with the owner Malek Ali for a chat.

Although it was very appealing, a million things went through my mind. Firstly, it was a start-up without a proven record. Secondly, could I do it? I had never presented a show although I have done radio and TV news, but these were highly scripted. I did want to learn how to be more impromptu. Thirdly, there would be a 30% pay cut. Lastly, IBM was a "secure" job. Remember that I had taken up coaching. I used this case study to coach with my fellow participants to arrive at a decision.

Firstly, financially my husband and I were stable and it was time for a change after being cocooned. He had achieved his dream of starting his own business and I was ready for something new. I figured that working in a business radio station as opposed to a music station would still be a relevant experience in the corporate world if everything went pear-shaped.

#BFMROCKS

Secondly, and this was nothing short of a miracle, I managed to get a two-year sabbatical from IBM (thanks Ali Munawar), which meant I could go back to IBM after two years if it didn't work out at BFM. So they were open

Hosting an event at work in 2018, an annual flagship event called Enterprise Breakaway.

to me being hired elsewhere while still paying for my medical and dental! I was truly blessed.

I was supposed to start in September 2008 when the station started but since I still had my 13th month bonus due, I ended up joining in January 2009 instead. Seriously, every obstacle (self-imposed mostly), was tackled and overcome. And so began another new interesting chapter in my life.

Well, two years passed and the station didn't close down. All kinds of personalities and cultures joined the station and because it's never been done before, obviously there were teething issues but I was not concerned because I still had the IBM trump card.

After the sabbatical was over, my eyes were opened to a bigger world out there beyond IBM or BFM.

To the outside world, that decision I made then didn't make sense. A pay cut with an unknown entity. However, I saw the potential in the station and felt great in being able to create a show called Enterprise covering entrepreneurship and personal development, which were topics very close to my heart. Every day was a learning experience. The joy of being able to do that was priceless. The friendships I have made with colleagues and guests have also been enriching and fulfilling.

Moral of the story is to work hard, know your job and always look at reskilling. My ex-boss, Julius Evanson from the PR consultancy, said there are only three rules. Firstly, the job is the only boss. Secondly, follow all instructions and thirdly, go the extra mile.

Life Lesson: Only you know what's best for you. Do a risk analysis on your life every so often and cover your bases. But sometimes, you need to listen to yourself and your True North will appear in the strangest ways.

With the wonderful team mates from BFM on our company
holiday in 2019.

STAGE 5

THE GROWING YEARS

The last decade definitely more than made up for the previous 10 years of being cocooned. I often wonder if the divorce was the catalyst for the many wonderful things I have accomplished, experienced and done. I believe the sense of my mortality came into clearer vision. I know I could not take physical things with me and that I would go naked, just how I arrived on this earth. It does give you a sense of urgency on life.

One of the few things I did not do when my marriage was crumbling and finally coming to a conclusion was to date. I was in no state of clarity and I did not want to jump into a relationship for the wrong reasons. I was very clear that I wanted to appreciate me and really there were other things to focus on then: my faith, my son, my fitness and my work. Most days, I came back from work, spent time with my son, exercised and spent time with God.

The concept of seasons in life did not make much sense to me until I experienced them myself. I felt like I had just come out of a long winter, in which even though I was building my mental, spiritual and physical muscles, I was still bundled up. Now, I felt like winter was over, spring was in the air and I was ready again to face the world.

In Tara Mohr's book, *Playing Big*, she says that women tend to hide and tell someone else's story. We can see the brilliance in others but not ourselves. My previous books have featured other people who have great stories to tell. I as a woman am almost embarrassed or shy to tell my own story, so this is the first one I have written about my life journey.

I was also hiding and I'll share some of my "strategies" which did not help me: the fear of speaking up, of rocking the boat, of displeasing others. Like many other women, these caused me to develop a number of "survival" behaviours, like conflict avoidance, self-censoring, people-pleasing, tentative speech and action. My biggest hiding strategy was sharing the brilliance of others while omitting my own, revealing my need to depend on other trusted authorities.

When thinking about writing my own story, I first tried to imagine my 80th birthday party, surrounded by family and friends. What would they say about me? If I wanted to be more macabre, what people would say about me at my funeral? I wrote down firstly what my son would say, and then my closest and dearest. I am hoping my son will say I was a wonderful mother. After that, what would people say about the life I have led and the kind of person I was? If I look at the Wheel of Life, what stories can I share in all these areas of my life?

In this period of life, I also saw friends who passed on way too young. What would I do differently about my life? I haven't lived for me in a long time: to exercise self-love and self-care, take time off for me and not have to explain myself to someone else. And really, I didn't have to. It was always always self-imposed. It's now more popular and acceptable to say these things.

Sometimes, we want to do something for ourselves and we label it as a "guilty" pleasure. There are days where I need a massage because I love myself and I need to relax. Why should

I be guilty about it? How can I love others if I can't love myself?

And so when I look at this last decade, it has been definitely a decade of growth and new experiences. I don't believe in the saying that life is short. Why would I impose that on myself? I say my life is abundant and I live accordingly. To all the new experiences from writing a book or running across Asia to Europe, I ask myself, why not and why not now?

I am putting this very simplistically. If the reason you can't do something is because of money, instead of ending that chapter, ask, how can I afford it? Don't hold back on what gives you joy because the joy you have will be poured into the lives of others. If your cup is overflowing, you can't help but give more.

How are you showcasing your life that is aligned with your values? When we talk about being congruent, are your thoughts, actions and behaviours aligned so that you can be truly authentic?

Every year, I set a theme for my life for that year. One year, it was saying yes to everything just like the movie, *Yes Man*. That was a funny year because I should have said no to some things, but still it was fun. One year it was Colourful and that year was colourful indeed. This year (the year of Covid-19), my goal is ironically Lightness. Just as well, it has already been a heavy year.

A conversation with a friend changed my theme. I had previously wanted Solid as my theme. My friend said everything about me is already solid. And any more solidness would make me heavier in spirit, actions and words. So with Lightness, if something or someone comes into my life that doesn't give me a light feeling, I shouldn't be associated with that person or thing.

Some questions you can ask yourself as you move forth in life. What achievements might help open doors for your career or move towards a new one? What accomplishments can you continue building on? What have you learned about yourself and your abilities that might inform you of your next steps? What are your short-term and long-term goals and how can you organise and prioritise them to keep you on your career path?

I am glad I have chosen Lightness as a theme. With a lot of things coming to a halt this year and thwarting some plans, we can only be light about things, otherwise I'd be getting my knickers in a twist over unmet goals. Now it's just to look at the goals and readjust to what feels right for the rest of the year. I am being as light-hearted and fluid as I possibly can.

I remember being 19 again, with that sense of adventure and excitement over what the future might hold. I am still big on having plans, goals, visions and dreams but at the same time, I am also ok if some things don't work. It's just God saying yes, no or not now. Readjust and realign again.

In the meantime, I am still alive doing other things I love like travelling whenever I can, making sure I have breaks when I can, because I know little breaks make me happy and allow me to reflect, rest, refocus, recharge and move again until the next rest stop.

I am a big fan of Arianna Huffington, the founder of *The Huffington Post* and now Thrive Global. She talks about micro steps we can take to change things. Have an adventure on one element of your Wheel of Life and it may not seem much in a year but over 10 years, your life would be highly enriched. People overestimate what can be done in one year, and underestimate what can be done in ten. We always overestimate the change that will occur in the short term and underestimate the change that will occur in the long term. Why don't you start now?

Better Not Bitter

Divorce. Here's that story again. I really don't like talking about it anymore, not because I am embarrassed or anything of that sort. It's just that I feel I've told it a million times but it is an important part of my life as I had to take the road less travelled. It became a crucible for the decisions I've made in the last decade. I do wonder sometimes whether the life I live right now would have happened if this did not happen. This definitely gave me a sense of urgency.

I remembered when he moved out, my whole world crumbled. It's not just a case of love lost. It was my identity not only as a wife, but a mother and a woman. It affected every aspect of my life. Even writing this is draining. I held on to this loveless marriage for six years because there was a son and shared homes involved.

I felt like a failure. It was as if everything I had done previously, from work to home, came to nought. This worthlessness permeated every aspect of my life. I lost my confidence as a woman. I second-guessed everything I did. Where did I go wrong? A wrong question to ask if you understand coaching.

Despite all the coaching courses and all the personal development books, there was no clarity on anything. I cried every night for months. My heart physically hurt. My young son saw his mother crying all the time and wondered what was happening. Food was tasteless. If it wasn't for my mother-in-law who stood by me and continued living with me long after the divorce, the home situation would have been worse. With her around, my son had some semblance of normalcy and stability.

The Kubler-Ross model identifies the five stages of grief: denial, anger, bargaining, depression and acceptance. Who knows how long each stage takes and just when you think you're past one stage, you find you have gone two steps back. People need to heal at their own pace. Well-meaning friends may wonder why it takes so long. If you find your friends cannot help or are tired of listening to your problems (everyone has problems of their own), please seek professional help. So long as you know you're making progress in one area of life, the rest will follow.

I spent a long time in denial, anger, bargaining and depression. I held on for six years, bargaining and hoping he would change his mind but it takes two hands to clap. Anger comes sometimes like a tsunami and sometimes in waves. Accept these feelings. Don't hide them (maybe in the privacy of your room). Never seek vengeance. Also, aim to be cordial at all costs for you and your children's sanity.

Not once did I have suicidal thoughts, as painful as it was. I knew I was on a downward spiral and could have gone down that path and had to do something about it, so I started exercising. I knew exercising would help me release happy chemicals. A much better solution than going to the pubs. People now look at me and think I have a wonderful social life. I do. But it wasn't the case for three years, when I pretty much cocooned myself in the comforts of my home after work.

In the book *Flourish* by Dr Martin Seligman, he talks about dealing with our issues and not in a flippant way. When we start taking depressive medication, it only takes care of 65% of the problem because these sorts of medications are cosmetic and not curative. So when we don't deal with the other 35% of our issues, it will crop up again in other ways. So seek the help of a coach or a therapist. I can't say that often enough.

I then brought all my troubles to God, all stages of denial. I had a simple prayer to God and that was for me to come out of this a better person, not bitter. I had no idea what better looked like without my husband in my life but I waited upon God. I was sure He encouraged me to exercise. I needed to take control back in my life. We have heard of areas within our control and areas beyond our control. I cannot control my ex-husband but I can control my own emotions and actions. I had to fill my cup again. Firstly, it was spiritual and now, fitness.

I remembered signing up for my first 10K. Less than six months before, I was someone who hadn't exercised for a long time, but I set my goal to finishing this 10K. Finishing it was more memorable than finishing my full marathon. Slowly but surely, I felt better. The situation had not changed but my mindset had.

And then I remembered the story of my father. Did I want to leave this world with the music still in me? What else did I want to do but didn't dare to do? I went on my first mission trip to Sri Lanka. Jaffna had just ended their decades-old civil war and you could see people living with such joy despite having so little.

I started thinking of all the places I wanted to visit "some day". I guess the day had arrived. I needed to find

In Sri Lanka on a church mission trip in 2019.

confidence in me again. And although the five stages of grief was initially meant for death, this whole experience felt like death to me because it was a loss I had to deal with. David Kessler wrote another book called *Finding Meaning: The Sixth Stage of Grief*. Yes, it was all about finding meaning in what has happened and making it meaningful.

I have never not been in a relationship of sorts since I was 15 so there I was in my forties learning to enjoy my company and to be whole again before I could be whole for anyone else who came into my life. Don't believe in romantic notions like needing someone to "complete" you.

Yes, I do have concerns about being alone but I also know being alone doesn't mean I have to be lonely. I am taking each day as it comes and trusting God will provide all that I need. I do have to say the last 10 years have been the most riveting of my life and I wonder if I would have taken the bull by the horns had this not happened.

Life Lesson: Always aim to be better, not bitter. Better is a much more joy-filled life.

Looking and Feeling Good is an Inside Job

I have always been conscious of my body. Growing up I had pockmarks on my legs from mosquito bites and allergies. Let's put it all out there. I was conscious of my weight as a teenager and I think basically all of my life. I wore dark clothes all the time and trousers ... all the time. Why? I was still conscious of my legs.

When I was 19 years old, my boobs became the next reason for my self-consciousness. When I was studying in Kuala Lumpur, mechanics wolf-whistled at me for two whole years. There was a deranged man who roamed the streets and every time he saw me, he would comment on my boobs. Once – this is still so vivid in my mind – I went to buy food and the mechanics were there having lunch together with other office workers. The deranged man shouted at me, "Big boobs girl!" I was wearing a baggy T-shirt but everyone turned to stare. So I remained strong and got my food. When I went back to my room, I started bawling.

So can you picture this? Conscious about my legs and my boobs. That's basically the whole body really. Don't

With the ex-bosses at Edelman, in my usual black outfit and not willing to stand out in a crowd then.

laugh. I hardly owned any dresses, everything was black and buttoned up. I know, looking at me now, you wouldn't believe it.

When was the wake-up call to be who I am? It was when I started feeling good about myself and establishing my identity.

Posing with the legendary Jimmy Choo, creator of bright, colourful shoes I felt good in.

I started buying dresses and no, no more black dresses. I needed to put some colour in my life. Putting on makeup made ME feel good. I decided I wanted to go to work in a happy mood so I put on the brightest dresses and the reddest lipstick. Was it a case of faking it until I made it? In a way, but I realised that I could decide, between the six inches of my head, what frame of mind I wanted to be in.

When I started meeting other men, I realised I was still attracting jerks into my life. Maybe I was overly suspicious after what I had been through, but I knew there were roadblocks when it came to relationships and there was something internal I needed to review.

I sought out my friend and coach Sheila Singam and when we went through timeline therapy, the words "I'm not good enough" came out. That was revelation. If my subconscious felt I was still not good enough, of course I was attracting the wrong sort into my life. We pick up baggage along the way on our journey in life. That baggage is not a childhood phenomenon but a disempowering belief that came about when my marriage was crumbling. So be aware of the rubbish you pick up along the way!

I have always struggled with a body image issue, and so I decided to get fit. I started working out a long time ago but always found it a challenge to lose the extra weight. After that session of realising that I thought "I'm not good enough", I also realised the emotional baggage could be translated into physical baggage.

This was only a couple of years ago. I decided not to worry about losing weight but getting rid of visceral fat which is dangerous for your health. That meant watching the food I ate, exercising, going for detox sessions and any non-invasive method I could get my hands on. My visceral fat went down 5% to normal levels and in the process I lost body fat and increased muscle content. Increased muscle content means more weight because muscle is heavier than fat.

So make sure you're measuring the right thing and doing something for the right reasons. The goal was to be fit, not thin. We are faced with so many unrealistic images today. Growing up, it was just female magazines but now we see them bombarded at us all the time online, where everything is Photoshopped.

People, mostly women, go through such great lengths to Photoshop themselves in real life. I want to look good too but within limits. The laugh lines are fine because it shows I have lived a life filled with experiences good and bad. At the end of the day, do what you must to feel good and not just to look good. If you do it to feel good, make sure it's for the long-term and not temporary because then you'll be looking for the next fix. Fix what you need to fix inside first.

I totally believe how a lot of emotional issues in life manifests in your physical health. Not so long ago, I developed a cough which lasted three weeks. My coach and friend Sheila coached me into realising there were some things I needed to say to someone; to get something off my chest literally and figuratively. After that very difficult conversation, there was a lot more clarity on my part although nothing was done. Miraculously though, my cough disappeared overnight.

I won't go into great detail here but a lot of life's issues, if not dealt with, manifests as issues in your body. The stress of these things will ultimately need to be released somewhere. That's where the word dis-ease came from – an unease in your life resulting in a disease. Everything connects!

Because of past experiences and words said to me, I was hiding my femininity for years. Don't be attractive because it will invite unwanted attention. Wear dark clothes to disguise the figure and unsightly body parts. I knew these things because of the books I've read and the numerous conversations I have had with experts, and yet I didn't think it would apply to me or affect me. How wrong can one be?

I physically and mentally felt lighter after that. My last book, *In Your Skin*, discussed being comfortable with who you are internally and externally. Internally is about how you feel and the career choices you make; externally is about how you feel which will translate into your own unique beauty.

Life Lesson: It may take a lifetime to peel the onion of life. Aim to get to your core, your authentic self.

The Tortoise and the Hare

I must have been running for about five years, happy to do my 10Ks or 12Ks. I found a new bunch of friends who were running freaks. Many had finished the full marathon (42K). I was impressed and intrigued and it was at the back of my mind.

I did a few 21Ks as a build-up but injured myself, though maybe it was more psychological. I decided I would take it easy because I really wanted to run for the long-term and I knew 10Ks were ideal for me.

Some of the friends I have made when running.

I never lost that dream of doing a full marathon. It was definitely an item on the bucket list. Then in 2015, I decided it was going to be THE year. There were several races to look at. I didn't want it to be at the end of the year because I'll be dragging my feet to train and dreading the whole year. I needed at least three months to train. I decided to sign up for the Gold Coast Airport Marathon. It's good to train in the humidity of Malaysia and run somewhere cooler. It never gets too cold at the Gold Coast, even during winter.

The other reason for running there was that I used to study in Queensland and had an old university mate living there, plus I wanted to visit other friends. Also, this particular marathon had a flat route. Hurrah!

What does it mean to train? Well, I didn't run every day, maybe three times a week. I worked out every day though. The weekends meant sleeping early and waking up even earlier to chalk up the mileage. I was so glad I decided to do a race in July and not at the end of the year. The plan was to get up to 30K during training and then taper off. The body is supposed to get used to long mileage. Well, I never got above 22K in my training. I think I did two half-marathons prior to the race and then a week before the race, I had major cramps.

All my friends said it was mind over matter. My ankle was telling me otherwise. I had one friend who would tease me and egg me on, telling me that I wouldn't finish the race since he knew that would just spur me. Other friends who had finished their marathons gave me other tips and tricks like keeping McDonald's salt packs in case I had cramps. Those came in handy.

So I arrived in Australia a day before the race and spent the day bracing myself. I got myself rocktaped and had my supplies of energy gels and salt packs in my race belt. The day started cool and true enough by 8am, the sun was heating up.

When the gun went off, everyone sped ahead of me. There were women who were twice my height and size walking faster than me. I refused to be deterred. My goal was to get to every checkpoint ahead of time or on time so that I would not be pushed into the sweeper bus for being behind time. It was probably in the third hour or so that I saw I was 30 minutes ahead of the scheduled time at the checkpoint so I could finally breathe a little sigh of relief. But I was only halfway through.

True enough, the cramps started coming in. Thank goodness for the salt packs. I also remembered my friend's face teasing me if I didn't finish. I just thought to myself, "Never again!" but I had to finish at least once so that I could claim to be a marathoner.

I finally caught up with the walking women at the 36th kilometre. Boy, do they walk fast or should I say, I run really slow. I walked the last two kilometres because I was cramping. There was hardly anyone around at the finishing line, but there was a good crowd of people along the route encouraging us.

After I collected my finisher medal, I didn't spend enough time cooling down and stretching properly, something I would regret in the next two days. There was this layer of salt on my body from my sweat. This wouldn't have happened in Malaysia because of the humidity, but I do have to say I am glad I did it in Australia. I am not sure if I can finish a race here in Malaysia.

In the next two days, I was as stiff as a board. I literally could not get up. I was walking like an Egyptian mummy. All the anti-inflammatory pills and painkillers had worn off and every step was excruciating and calculated.

What was it like finishing a marathon? It is one of the most fulfilling experiences in my life. I am so glad I did it. When you have finished a marathon, you feel invincible and that you can achieve anything in the world. I do have to say, painful as it was, that it's mind over matter. The lessons I learned then were: to finish what I start, that I've got more in me than I possibly can imagine, to always do my homework and preparation and that it pays to be persistent and consistent.

I've now been running since 2010 and yes I'm sticking to my 10Ks. I just want to be able to do this for the rest of my life. I have said vehemently that I will never do a full marathon again, not so much because of the race itself but the preparation before which takes time and effort. I'm not sure I'm willing to make that sacrifice again. This would mean an opportunity cost for doing something else instead and right now I have other priorities and interests.

Finishing my one and only full marathon ... for now?

This was a big one to have checked off the bucket list. I not only got the T-shirt but a medal. Five years have passed since I did that run. Would I do it again? After all, I vowed never to do a 21K either but I did one last year. Please don't tempt me! A bribe might work though ...

Life Lesson: You never know what you're made of until you extend yourself. Don't be in a hurry for that dopamine hit every day. Delayed gratification, persistency and consistency are old and trusted virtues.

Multiply Your Talents

It was my friend in PR who asked me to write a book. What should I write about? What do I have to offer? Who would want to buy it? Who am I to write a book? Yes, we all go through fears in trying something new. I also like a good challenge. And I started asking different questions.

What if it worked? What if people liked it? What's the worst that can happen? What have I got to lose? Most of the time, when trying something new, I ask myself, firstly, whether I would learn something new from it and secondly, would I literally die from it? If I won't and I don't affect other people's lives, I'm usually game for something that intrigues me.

So I decided to self-publish my first book, *PR Yourself*. I was very fortunate that I had a few people support me financially, including my boss, Malek Ali. And so, after six months of work, it was finally out. No fancy book launch, but I was happy. Along with the book publishing came speaking. For people thinking about writing books, be prepared to promote it. And that's where speaking comes in. Popular Books, a bookstore and publishing house, asked me to speak at their book events to promote the book. Usually there won't be many people there but it makes for great practice.

Again, it was outside my comfort zone. People assume because I work in radio I could speak. Interviewing for print, radio and TV are all different skills actually. In radio, you have to capture a person's attention by the way you speak and the energy you emit auditorily, putting colours in words. In radio, I am having a conversation with someone and usually my guest is speaking more than me. In TV, there are more considerations like how you look while holding a conversation.

In emceeing, the event is the star of the show and you have to make sure you keep time and feel the energy of the room. There are intricacies in the things you say if there's a launch gambit and

Moderating one of many corporate events.

you have to quickly bounce back should something go awry. In moderating events, you have to know your topic and make sure there's rapport with the person you're interviewing.

When it comes to speaking, it's about reading the crowd and how you use the extra space given to you because you own the space. This is in addition to getting your points across in a succinct and energetic way. The energy is also different depending on the size of the crowd, the size of the space and the duration of the talk.

Covid-19 made a lot of people jump on the webinar bandwagon. I was also one of them. Again, another different set of skills. There's promotion of the webinar before and after it's taken place (the PR skills learned many years ago help). When you are doing the webinar, you have to make sure you keep the audience engaged and people can come in and out whenever they feel like it. The one thing I haven't ventured into is acting and comedy. Is it on the bucket list? Not really, but I won't say no, and will try it out once just for the experience.

Even with writing, there are different kinds of writing. Are you writing an article or are you writing a book? If you are writing a book, what sort of book? If you are writing an article, the length of the article will also determine the style of the writing. All this with the audience in mind. After writing five books, I've learned that every experience is still different. I have since worked with another book publisher, MPH Publishing, and learned that the requirements are different for different publishers. I would like to think I have improved since the first book.

I am also trained as a coach and from that role, I've learned that there are always new tools and skills to improve on if you want to grow with your clients and be of constant value-add to the people around you.

One of the lessons in the Bible is about multiplying your talents. Matthew 25:15 says, "And to one he gave five talents, to another two, and to another one, to each according to his own ability." God has given us all talents and He will multiply them if we use them and put them into practice. No time for false modesty. I truly believe we all have talents and the world needs them.

Is it fear or awe holding us back? Jonathan Fields talks about the Hebrew words for fear which are *pachad* and *yirah*. *Pachad* is "projected or imagined fear", the "fear whose objects are imagined." That is what we might think of as lizard brain fear: the fear of horrible rejection that will destroy us or the fear that we will simply combust if we step out of our comfort zones.

Yirah is the fear that shows up in those moments when we uncover a dream, access our real feelings about an important situation, or contemplate taking a big leap toward a more authentic life. So which is holding you back? *Pachad* or *yirah*?

Here are some questions for your reflection. You can ask yourself what type of job you would want if salary weren't a factor. How do you define a successful career? How does your definition of a successful career relate to your values? Think about who your work is aimed at supporting or the lives you hope to impact. For example, do you want to help entrepreneurs, refugees, families, working mothers, people with learning disabilities or millennials?

What skills do you currently have that can help you and what skills and qualifications might you have to develop? You can also ask yourself questions about the kind of life you would like and how the career you want might impact that. You might envision working from home or travelling around the world. Both of these ambitions might also affect whether you have or want a family.

Taking that big leap means leading a more authentic life. When you take that simple first step, other doors will open. Maybe the word leap frightens you; then just take a step forward, one foot at a time.

One simple step has led me to many steps and opportunities. I am glad I took that first step. Matthew 25:19 says, "For to everyone who has, more will be given, and he will have abundance; but from him who does not have, even what he has will be taken away." Use it or lose it.

Life Lesson: You won't know until you try. One opportunity leads to another. Experiment and try new things.

The World Doesn't Revolve Around You

I held back on fun in my twenties and thirties thinking it'll happen one day. Travel is MY thing as I am sure it is with many people. There is so much you can learn from travelling; not just the destination itself but also the preparation.

Being on a plane or a helicopter is nothing new to me. We would fly back to Kuching when I was living in Brunei. The major holiday the family took was when I was five and my father won the lottery. We travelled to West Malaysia and Singapore. And then when I was about 13, my father took his daughters for holidays which were a bit further away. He didn't take the sons because his logic was that he had already given them property.

But I knew he just liked being with his girls. We went to Hong Kong, Taiwan, Korea and Japan and that was a huge deal.

My big trip after that was leaving for Australia for university. In my twenties and thirties, we did annual holidays and looking back, I did travel quite a lot. But when there were plans to go further, I always told myself, someday in the future.

And then in my forties, I set a goal to visit two new countries a year. That would involve both time and money, so I had to be resourceful in earning more money. Just imagine, if I did that over 10 years, I would have been to 20 new countries, and even then would have barely scratched the surface.

There are some places I go to over and over again. One of these is Bali. Bali never disappoints. I always do things on repeat for a few days, like massages and sipping cocktails as the sun sets. It's a place close enough to go regularly. That's my personal haven.

It's only been in the last 10 years that I got serious about my travel. What else was I waiting for? In preparing for a trip, you always plan for the right time to make your bookings. I plan for my holidays at the beginning of the year and slot work around those days. I have noticed that when I don't plan a date, things will happen.

People also tend not to carve out time to have fun in their lives. For the longest time I was wracked with guilt when I had fun but now I know it's important for me to refresh, reflect and renew. It makes work fun knowing I have something to look forward to. And after a break, I look forward to going back to work.

I have travelled with friends and also gone on solo trips. I have fears just like everyone else but I find myself getting more courageous with every trip. I still have a fear of missing a connecting flight, especially in a country where people don't speak English. I also hate going through immigration. I always feel like a criminal!

One of my favourite trips was to Greece. We had finished Athens and were heading to Meteora, a UN World Heritage Site with monasteries on top of hills. In the past, the monks would go up using a basket. I had read about it. Who knew I would get to visit it? The journey involved driving by the beautiful Aegean Sea, making a stop at any town the moment we felt hungry.

It was the end of the summer and so most restaurants were closed when we drove into this town. I still to this day can't remember the name of the place but I definitely remember Ulya. We saw one restaurant open and so we sat there. This lady with the kindest face came out to greet us with hardly any English. We were the only guests.

She started giving us extra dishes and said they were "on the house!" She brought us into the kitchen and showed us her olive garden in the back. When it came to dessert, we only ordered one portion because we were full but she made sure all of us got a piece. Of course we tipped her well. Before we left, I whispered to my friends that this won't be the end of freebies. True enough, as I left the toilet, she pulled out a huge bottle of drinking water and said with her broken English, "For the road."

How can you forget the love? It wasn't the beautiful island of Santorini, the monumental Parthenon or the majestic Meteora that made that trip the most significant. When people ask me what has been my most memorable holiday, I think of that trip because of the universal language called love, spoken without words but actions, sign language and genuine smiles.

What will travelling teach you? Heaps, if you let it. It will teach you to be alert and wary, and be exposed to many people. Croatia was just as amazing as Greece but there was one horrible experience with a rude lady and a reminder that people are the same everywhere, with our baggage and attitudes.

Most of the time getting lost in translation is half the fun. I shudder to think what it will be like without Google Translate but I have travelled without that too. Learning to adjust and be adaptable and knowing sometimes it's ok to let go and laugh at ourselves, like the time we missed a bus back to another town in Croatia. Thank goodness we had buffered in another day without missing a connecting flight or transportation. Thank goodness it was also a problem that money can solve!

When I look at the people living around me, fellow Malaysians and foreigners alike, I have a better understanding of who they are and find myself able to connect with them on a personal and intimate level, to see the world through their eyes. You can always find a connection to everyone around you if you want to because values like family and love are universal.

Life Lesson: Combine growth and fun through travel. We're so small in the scheme of things and travelling humbles you if you let it.

Create Your Own Press ... But Don't Believe It

I am often asked to speak or talk on personal branding. It's something that I consciously do for professional reasons. Many people are embarrassed about the concept of personal branding. Let me address what it is from an external perspective. You are what Google says you are. It's your unique selling proposition and a decision whether people want to hire you or not. Perception

Part of a judging panel in 2018 of Chivas Regal's The Venture, which celebrates social enterprises around the world.

is reality and who's controlling the narrative.

Let me talk about misconceptions now. No, you don't have to be an extrovert to build your brand. No, you won't lose your privacy. Will your weaknesses be revealed? Depends on how you look at it. Reading this book thus far, you will see my many flaws and it is important that you know who I really am because authenticity is key.

Is it scary and intimidating? No, it doesn't have to be. Talking about the work you do is not bragging. You have a gift and the world needs to know about it. My pastor once talked about false modesty. He said he wanted to be a great pastor. And he asked the congregation if he wanted the people to say if he was a great pastor. He said obviously. So enough with the false modesty. If we are good at something, be proud of the fact that you are bestowed with certain talents. Own it boldly. You don't have to be conceited or arrogant about it though.

Granted, personal branding doesn't mean just talking about yourself without merit and content. A brand is a promise that you make to your target audience and ultimately, how your audience perceives you. You may not be a product but you may be an employee. So how does your employer or future employer perceive you? Amazon's Jeff Bezos said, "Your brand is what people say about you when you're not in the room."

People will feel an emotional connection to your brand by how you have added value to their lives. Most memorable brands inspire, empower, enlighten, entertain and educate. Do you reflect the same values at every touchpoint? That means not only the products or services you provide but also how you respond to an email or how you treat others. It's all part of the brand!

Earlier, I mentioned this book by Tara Mohr, *Playing Big*. That was such an eye-opening book and I saw that some of the constraints we impose on ourselves, especially women, are universal, not just an Asian thing like I thought. Here are some myths and beliefs most of us have grown up with.

Mohr mentions "The Good Girl" syndrome. When we are in school, we get recognised for our efforts. When we get to work, we may or may not be recognised for our efforts other than what we see in our yearly reviews. What then? Most of us just stay mousey and hope to be recognised one day. Let's leave our good student habits behind and talk about our efforts because no one else will.

She also talks about hiding strategies where we always give what sounds like valid excuses not to play a bigger game. Excuses like needing another degree (but not having the time) or waiting for the children to grow up before getting started (even when there are many possible and micro steps to getting started). Instead of spending my time during Covid-19 watching Netflix, I got started on this book. There is a Malay saying, *sedikit-sedikit lama-lama jadi bukit,* which loosely translated means: if you build at something long enough, it becomes a hill after a while.

We all have an inner critic, this voice that tells you a million things. One of the most common one is: "You aren't ready yet." Ready for what? If something comes along, do you question yourself or convince yourself that you need more time to prepare or that you need more experience?

According to a Hewlett Packard internal report, men apply for a job when they meet only 60% of the qualifications, but women apply only if they meet 100% of them. The only thing holding women back is the lack of confidence and not the skills.

I for one am most game about things nowadays because of this new-found knowledge. How else will I get the experience otherwise? The only way to replace fear is to have courage and do it anyway. You will find that confidence builds the more often you raise your hand to do something.

Let me share a very recent experience. I used to do a lot of moderating and emceeing work, but a lot of this has been shelved temporarily because of Covid-19. Well, I need to be relevant and so I started doing more webinars because that's the way now and the way forward. Some interesting propositions from clients have happened because they have seen me still moderating on other mediums. Did I have any experience before? Not really, I just thought it was fun to try something new and voila!

I want to share the concept of leaping mentioned by Tara Mohr. It's a new way of thinking and a new way of acting. It's closely related to the concept used in design thinking called prototyping.

Pandemic or no pandemic, it's off to work. With Khairy Jamaluddin (second from left), Malaysia's Minister of Science, Technology & Innovation, in 2020.

For example, if you're thinking of writing a book over the year, why not start with an article and see if it resonates with your audience? If you're thinking of spending six months on developing a workshop, why don't you conduct a pilot mini-workshop in two weeks' time and learn from your RSVPs the kind of people you're attracting? It's no skin off your nose for trying.

My life has been a series of leaps and bounds. One leap usually leads to another leap or not at all. If I didn't try, I wouldn't know. Sometimes by trying something, you will see whether you're on the right trajectory or not. If it's right, other doors will open. If it's not, you will have lots of stories. In an online world, where your details are shared through Google in mere seconds, don't let the acclaim get to you either. Don't believe your own press. Stay humble always.

Why am I sharing this with you and why do I think personal branding is important? Build yourself whether you're an entrepreneur or working in an organisation. Whether someone hires you depends on how well they know you or of you. You can develop your brand and your story by design or by default. You can control the narrative. There is a lot of material out there on techniques but first you need the conviction as to why it's important. Don't hide or keep what you've been gifted with. So why don't you take that leap?

Life Lesson: You have a great deal of control over the way you are perceived. Your brand represents a strong sense of who you are, what you stand for, what you most want to be known for and your legacy.

You Don't Know What You Don't Know ... That's How You Grow

Recently I was asked to share life experiences with a few women who had embarked on a career comeback programme because they had lost their jobs, were planning to rejoin the workforce after a hiatus or plotting a career switch. I shared my life journey and also the many things I have tried as I have outlined in this book.

One particular woman said she was an introvert and didn't know how to take

Meeting interesting people like Jimmy Wales, co-founder of Wikipedia (what will we do without it?).

things forward when I offered some suggestions to improve on her resume. I said, we can't attempt to know it all and it's easy to use our personality or disposition as a reason not to move forward. The world has changed so much and if we don't take the next step, however small, to improve or evolve, who can we blame?

I have over the years conducted more than 5,000 interviews with the likes of Simon Sinek, HRH Prince Andrew, the late Stephen Covey and former Finnish Prime Minister Alexander Stubb. What are my experiences with them and who is my favourite? It's like asking who's my favourite child. Most have been over the phone and some I have had the privilege to meet face-to-face.

Some of the most memorable include the infamous Julian Assange of Wikileaks, who was in Malaysia before heading out to Sweden and subsequently getting into trouble. He was confident he would be safe when I asked him if he thought the law would catch up with him. Then there was HRH Prince Andrew's assistant who wasn't too pleased when I took too many photos. The late Jack Welch, who was touted the greatest CEO for many years when he headed General Electric, still had the gusto and energy in his voice even though he was in his eighties.

Rubbing shoulders with Halle Berry in LA, at the finals of global competition, The Venture.

Some interviewees exuded warmth and some were mechanical. Motivational speaker Nick Vujicic came in with a large filming crew and despite the many people in the studio, made you feel like he was only talking to you. He prayed over me at the end of the interview in the studio. To this day, this is one of the most touching experiences I have had.

I sometimes forget to count my lucky stars. I am so fortunate to have had the opportunities to speak to so many people. These interviews look great on my profile, but more importantly, I can say for sure that I have learned from everyone I have spoken to – from big names to up-and-coming entrepreneurs – and also, over time, become less awestruck. There is not a single day that I have not learned something new.

Other legends I have spoken to include Martin Cooper, who while working at Motorola invented the mobile phone in the 1970s. When I spoke to him, I could hear his excitement like he only invented it yesterday. The late Ralph Baer, known as the Father of Video Games, helped spark this multi-billion dollar industry. He taught me about the importance of having fun and being creative despite being a radical game-changer.

What I love most about all these stories is their "a-ha" moment when they are onto something. I want that infectiousness in my life. Almost always, the story includes a turning point, obstacles and of course, persistence and belief in what they are doing. I look out for what could be their secret ingredient and this sparks joy in what I do. Curiosity never killed the cat.

I sometimes have to be reminded of all these names I have had the honour of meeting and speaking to. There are a lot more on my wish list. Women who have broken the mould, like Arianna Huffington of *The Huffington Post* fame, former First

Lady Michelle Obama and Spanx's founder Sara Blakely. I am putting it out there now; who knows, right?

It's not only the big names that excite me. I get motivated from hearing entrepreneurs who have gone against the grain, especially in these trying times. A most recent story is Leron Yee of DKing, a durian and durian product supplier who sold 300,000 yuan of durians in China in 10 minutes thanks to the Internet and shared a story of how durians do very well in Hong Kong because a lot of people there believe the Musang King durian can cure Covid-19. If only this were true!

There is a young girl called Shirley Chai who quit her corporate job to start her own artisanal soy sauce using non-GMO soybeans. Musees is her own brand but she is capitalising on her family business which has been around since 1957 (as old as Malaysia). How can one not be inspired and learn from a story like that? I sometimes get more excited hearing about these humble stories than those from the big names.

You don't know what you don't know. That's how I choose to operate. That's how I stay enthusiastic, curious, naive and child-like because who knows what tomorrow brings. The opposite characteristic would be boredom, jadedness and being burdened by experience. I am choosing to change the map of my world to make it more wondrous and large.

Life Lesson: Instead of being fixed in our ways and thinking, be prepared to have your mind blown and perspectives changed.

EPILOGUE –
THERE ISN'T ONE

An epilogue is a final or concluding act or event. To quote Lenny Kravitz, it ain't over till it's over. I feel I have barely scratched the surface of what life has to offer. Mindsets and reframes, I can't talk enough about them. I stand by my conviction that you can have everything in life ... just maybe not all at the same time. Let me share some of my reframes.

I don't like saying life is short. We tend to say this when you hear of the demise of friends at a young age. By claiming life is short, it's like a self-fulfilling prophecy. I like to say my life is abundant and then live accordingly. Regardless of the amount of time that is given, each day is abundant to me. Have I lived fully each and every day? There is a sense of urgency in everything I do. It may sound a little macabre but I would like to know that I have lived each day fully. If I have scheduled a break to have fun, I do that wholeheartedly and joyfully too.

I organised a webinar recently on the topic of guilt. We feel guilty for having fun and call it guilty pleasures. Why should I feel guilty when I go for a massage, get a pedicure or a facial? These things give me comfort and relaxation. Make time for yourself. Make time for self-love and self-care. When you're a happy woman, people around you will be happy. A happy mother makes for a happy child.

There are a couple of things you can quit doing. Quit worrying about what people think. To quote Rupaul, "Unless they paying your bills, pay them bxxxxes no mind!" We stop ourselves even before we start because we are so busy thinking about what people would think. Really, everyone's life is full; most times, people are too busy to notice us.

When I went to the Money & You seminar years ago, we talked about feelings. All feelings are equal. People expect to see people happy all the time. The reality is that people aren't. Quit denying anger, sadness and fear. There are many times I feel these things. I acknowledge these feelings, express it out (maybe shouting into a pillow is a better idea) and address it.

Why am I angry? Why am I sad? Why am I afraid? Ask yourself "why" five times in a particular situation – with each answer, you will get deeper to the crux of the matter. And when I get to the heart of the matter and know exactly why I'm feeling a particular way, I then make plans to do something about it.

This leads into my next point which is to quit blaming. The moment we blame, we become a victim. Yes, I understand you want to rant sometimes. I do too. I let it fester for a while if I need to and then I can look at things logically. When they first announced the Movement Control Order during Covid-19, I was angry that my freedom was taken away and my two holiday plans were cancelled. Yes, I was behaving like a spoilt child. And then, once I had finished with my pity party, I looked at the things I could do instead, and found that I quite enjoyed the quiet time!

Women take such pride in being multi-taskers. We wear it like a badge of honour. Because you're putting 20% in five things, you will not be able to give each thing your full 100%. Don't overfunction. Be realistic in what you can do. Not every gap in your diary needs to be filled. In fact, put in your diary time to do nothing so that you can think freely. We are human beings, not human doings.

As one of the 10 commandments in the Bible says, "You shall not covet your neighbour's house. You shall not covet your neighbour's wife, or his male or female servant, his ox or donkey, or anything that belongs to your neighbor" (Exodus 20:17). In a nutshell, don't compare and don't look over your shoulder. You can't move forwards if you have your eyes looking in the rear mirror.

Comparing yourself to others will usually stop you in your tracks. If it makes you feel inferior, then that's not a good sign. If it inspires you to be better, however, then let it serve as fuel to better yourself. Remember, we are all made differently with different talents and gifts. Your goal is to unearth these talents, use them and you'll find it gets multiplied into other areas you never knew you liked or were good at. The idea is just to start and experiment. If it works out, great. If it doesn't, put it down as experience and have a good laugh about it.

Humour. Never lose your sense of humour in this journey called life. When things happen, we have that moment to decide whether we want to absorb that information. Viktor Frankl, Austrian neurologist, psychiatrist, Holocaust survivor and author of *Man's Search For Meaning*, identified three main ways of realising meaning in life: Creative Values, by making a difference in the world; Experiential Values, by experiencing something or encountering someone; and Attitudinal Values, by adopting a courageous and exemplary attitude in situations of unavoidable suffering. Yes, attitude is key!

As you are embarking on ways to make changes in your life, remember it can be done with micro steps. Bad habits are difficult to break. One of my tricks is not to remove it but to replace it with something else. Don't beat yourself up if things don't happen overnight, because they won't. Please also don't forget to celebrate when you experience victories, big or small.

BONUS TRACKS

Mental Real Estate

Multitasking is the enemy of deep, intellectual thought. We are sometimes afraid of our own thoughts and to reflect deeply on all aspects of life. We mask it by doing something and think busyness is productive. I heard this analogy once. When we were young, we were worried about monsters under the bed, but when we shine a torchlight under the bed, there is no monster. So if there are anxieties in the deep recesses of your mind, shine a light on them, address them and you will see there are no monsters at all.

I have just bought all of Dr Caroline Leaf's books. If you haven't read any of her stuff, I highly recommend her books about how the brain works. She explains how we are able to change our brains for the better and it affects everything in our lives: mind, body and spirit. I am going to refer to one of her "easier" books, *Switch On Your Brain*, where she uses the term "mental real estate". Picture this for a moment: You want your real estate to grow in value. So what are you doing to add value to it? Well, you don't want squatters living there for one! When you're spending time gossiping, whinging and whining, does it add to the real estate?

Yes, we love time with our girlfriends and having a good chat. As much as possible, keep things uplifting and encouraging. As much as possible, also know your boundaries and capabilities. There are people we want to support and we should do so as much as possible. But after a certain point, if you are not a trained psychiatrist, refer people to professional help. This is putting boundaries for your real estate. Sometimes people just want to vent and don't expect a solution from you. I know I have friends I can count on to vent at and to listen to my concerns and worries. That's the first category.

Now the second category. Sometimes people come to me for advice and I put on my coaching hat and we co-create solutions. It's great when advice is taken and people take the next steps. I have a friend who is a coach. I will ask her to turn on her "coach mode" and we get together to work through my issues (payment is a meal in this case!).

The third category is the one that drains me. We sometimes have friends who are constantly venting and have constant issues in their lives which sound like a broken record. Same sxxx, different day. We hear this drama on constant repeat. In Neuro Linguistic Programming, this is called a secondary gain. They don't want to resolve the issue because this way, they get constant attention. The secondary gain seems more important than the primary gain which is to resolve the constant problem.

I would at this point lovingly but firmly point them in the right direction for assistance because I am not trained as a psychiatrist and a coach can only help when the individual really wants to solve the issue. I have to draw boundaries to protect my mental real estate, otherwise I will get dragged into the misery. Yes, it's cruel to be kind but I have to think of my own self-preservation and sanity. This is my point about squatters taking up my mental real estate.

These are energy vampires. If you have seen the comedy TV series, *What We Do In The Shadows*, the character Colin Robinson does just that. He gets the energy from others by boring everyone with his inane conversation and although this may not be the case in my third category, you get the picture. Be careful too, misery loves company!

Now, knowing that your mental real estate has great value and this value can increase with care and upgrades, what are you doing to nourish your brain and your mind? Feed it with positive thoughts and read uplifting as well as educational books. Your brain scientifically grows if you challenge it intellectually, regardless of age.

We are constantly bombarded with information online. How much information we are fed with and how much the brain can process varies from 60 to 120 bits per second. Shouldn't we ensure that the information that comes in nourishes us and is as beneficial as possible?

In all this, I also know my personality type. I can get easily flustered and recognise that in myself and that is why I seek ways to prevent getting flustered. When something bothers me, I try not to react immediately. I take some time to process what has happened and then work on the best possible solution. Reacting immediately has had its negative repercussions.

Are you the sort that is easily flustered or does it take a lot to ruffle your feathers? If you're the "cool as a cucumber" sort, I envy you! I am naturally not and that's why when something does not align with me, I keep quiet and process the information at my pace. The "Intel Inside" needs processing time. This realisation has come about because many relationships have been negatively impacted thanks to me flying off the handle all too easily. With time comes clarity in my case.

Nourishing your mental real estate can be as easy as eating food, getting a sun tan, giving a compliment while eating dark chocolate! These are simple life hacks. That's why I try exercising the first thing in the morning and preferably outdoors as it sets my mood for the whole day. Put the odds in your favour for a great day. You can't pour from an empty cup, so fill it up.

I am writing this chapter in Kota Kinabalu, Sabah, on the wonderful island of Borneo. Later, I am going for a swim! For now, where is the chocolate?

Giving and Receiving

It's always better to give than to receive. Yeah, right. I know it's hard to fathom but it's actually true. Call it karma, call it the universe but I'll call it God. In the Bible, Exodus 23:19a quotes, "The best of the first fruits of your ground you shall bring into the house of the Lord your God." Regardless of your beliefs, I have heard countless stories of people getting more because they gave. Maybe it's because of your gratitude that somehow attracts good back into your life.

It started as a social experiment with a small sum of RM50 as a monthly contribution to World Vision in my twenties. I liked the work they did and although it's presented as sponsoring a child, it's actually about providing for the village the child belongs to and the goal is ultimately self-sustainability before they move on to another village. Since I didn't have the time to physically help, the least I could do was provide financially. I would receive regular updates on how the child was doing.

And then, with every annual pay raise, I would increase the number of children I could sponsor. One of the causes I believe in is children's education so that every child can have a better chance of a better life. I feel a crucial element of giving is not expecting anything back in return. And then, I got more adventurous. I actually decided to tithe 10% of my earnings to my church. Gasp! That's a lot of money. The oddest thing is, I never realised I was missing it when I started giving it. And through the years, I have always been provided for in more ways than one.

There are causes I believe in as I have matured. I give talks about the initiatives of social enterprises and programmes to empower women. I am also now an ambassador for Women of Global Change KL, with the mission to increase the number of women in businesses by 40% in 2030 from its current 20%. A Big Hairy Audacious Goal (BHAG), but why not? I believe when women are financially independent, they are empowered to do more. Here in Malaysia, we have Dignity for Children, that helps the marginalised community in Malaysia gain an education. I have sent my son there to be a volunteer so that he can see how privileged he is.

I have also gone to Sri Lanka for church mission work. The needs there are different, and I also need to see how privileged I am in this part of the world. Sometimes we need reminders of the many blessings we have and it's really good for my soul. Sri Lanka always has a special place in my heart. As little as they have, when you visit them, there is first and foremost, the all-important cup of tea, after which they will try to feed you with the mountain of rice prepared. In my mind, I am thinking of all the carbohydrates I shouldn't be consuming! On a serious note, how do people who have so little materially, have so much to give? What generous and loving hearts.

After 20 years of sponsoring children with World Vision, I am now one of the ambassadors for their WASH (Clean Water & Sanitary Hygiene) pillar. This has opened my eyes to how a lack of access to clean water affects a child's life. When girls travel for miles to collect water, sometimes they get attacked along the way. The time spent collecting water also means time away from school. And here we are, just turning on the tap and we have clean water.

I have also discovered a social enterprise farm in the Philippines where the "Bright Poor" boys learn how to run a farm and start businesses. These are boys who are bright but because they have not had any opportunity in life, are now given a chance to make something of their lives. Gawad Kalinga, which was started by Tony Meloto, hopes that boys will not have to go to the cities, end up in vice and live in slums. There wouldn't be a need to move to the cities if opportunities were available where they are.

I sent my son there for two weeks working on a farm when he was 15. He made new international friends and saw how they lived. When I asked him what he learned, it wasn't what I expected. He couldn't wait to return because everyone spoilt him as

As a supporter of World Vision for over 20 years, I was really honoured when they asked me to be an ambassador.

a foreigner. Biggest lesson for him was that Filipinos were funny! This was not what I had in mind, but I hope the seeds of giving have been planted.

There is always a need in every community. Open your eyes to what's happening around you. What's the point of my sharing all this? Giving has worked for me and in my small way I feel I have played a part. Your giving may be in your time or skills. We all live in a community and if we can do something nice and good, it makes a difference to someone's life. This is the story of the boy throwing the starfish back into the sea: he threw one starfish at a time even though there was a whole load lying by the beach. Focus on the one in hand and work from there.

Opportunities that have come my way have benefitted me a hundredfold in so many areas. I don't think I am more special than the person next to me. My mum once said when you're holding on to things so tightly your fist is held closely. When it's held so tightly shut, you can't get things anyway. You have to open that fist to give and to receive.

Don't get stressed about the issues of the world. It sometimes looks far-reaching and impossible where we are. Some things lie in areas beyond our control but some things are in areas within control. We all can change the world by helping one person at a time. You'll get a hit of oxytocin which is good for your health in the process!

Pull Your Trigger

I have often looked back on my life and to the unkeen eye and the outside world, the last 10 years have been most exciting. Online media does make it seem terribly glamorous, doesn't it?

Be a game changer wherever you are.

I get asked two very popular questions whenever I am being interviewed. One of them is: "What is your greatest achievement so far?" It makes me think, but I really don't think it's a fair question. There are so many aspects of my life and it hasn't been one great achievement that has made me what I am. Also, there are some things I am still trying to achieve.

I look at my life in segments and compartments and I have been "successful" in various areas. We're all multifaceted individuals and I am a sum of many parts. If you look at the Wheel of Life, there are various aspects: faith, fun, finance, fitness, family, friendships, community, mental, relationships and career. When I am asked what my greatest achievement is, the interviewer is usually referring to my career achievements. I take this opportunity to clarify that success is not only

All children should have access to education. it's a basic human right.

measured in terms of career success.

In the area of faith, having gone on several mission trips to Sri Lanka is success to me. From the area of fun, having travelled the world incorporating runs, concerts and sightseeing is important to me. From the area of fitness, to be in the best shape possible is a yearly goal and of course, finishing one full marathon. From the area of finance, to have a certain amount of money in the bank.

From the area of family, it is that my son will turn out to be an independent young man who loves his mummy and from the area of friendships, that I have meaningful friendships with different kinds of people. From the area of community, my work with World Vision.

From the area of mental, that I continue to learn something new every year that makes me uncomfortable and to read many books. From the area of career, it's still an on-going attempt to be the best I can be as a communicator. And from the area of romantic relationships, I am still working on finding the right person. These goals change and get improved upon so there's no one thing that has helped me entirely in this life journey.

On to the other question, which is: "What is the one challenge that you have overcome to make you where you are today?" I always talk about the divorce as the trigger but then looking back over the years, I realised there have been many triggers, as I have shared in this book.

I believe all these triggers have prepared me for the unplanned. One trigger is leaving Brunei at 14 and the only world I knew. I hated it then but then I also got familiar and comfortable about change and learned to make new friends. Watching my dad lose his job taught me about the working world, to always have a side hustle and the importance of passive income.

Doing a live TV show was not something I planned either but because I took the risk, it led the way for me into broadcasting. Trying out network marketing gave me an avenue to earn passive income and to understand rejection. That experience taught me humility.

In my twenties, I worked three jobs at the same time to make ends meet: I worked in a PR consultancy, presented the news and was a part-time lecturer. I learned presentation skills and dreamed of a future buying a home with other comforts. I wanted to know how far I could stretch myself. Trust you me, none of my peers were doing these things in their spare time.

When I had my son, it taught me about being responsible for another person's life. That to me is one of the scariest things in life, to nurture someone. Travelling alone is also something that I am not comfortable with. Will I be safe? Will I like my own company?

When I wrote my first book, I took the self-publishing route. It wasn't easy raising funds to write the first book. Who would support me? What if it didn't sell? What if people laughed at me? What if I had nothing intelligent to say? What gave me the right to write this book? Guess what? I did it anyway. It opened the doors for me as a speaker and I became regarded as a subject matter expert. I didn't die from that experience. It helped build my confidence.

Have they all been successful activities? Not everything, obviously. Like the DJ, guitar, pole-dancing (yes, seriously) and singing courses I didn't finish. Or my attempts at jewellery making (I didn't like dealing with fire in silversmithing). Overall, they were fun ventures because I choose to look at them as fun learning experiences. My heart wasn't in them but I learned about the mechanics of these skills and enjoyed the journey. They gave me more fodder to talk about things.

Why do I feel this is so important? Don't wait for that one big thing to happen before you head in a different trajectory. Be prepared. Use every little moment as teaching moments in preparation of what might or might not happen. Where in the Wheel of Life are you feeling lethargic and need a boost or a change? Yes, we all live full and busy lives and think we don't have time. We all have the same amount of time; carve out the time so that you continue to evolve and grow. Most of the time, you have to pull your own triggers to be uncomfortable so that you will grow. Go ahead, make your day!

A Spoonful of Courage and Bucketloads of Effort

As I write some of the life lessons in this book here, a friend who reviewed my book said it was important to share where I came from so that I could really connect with a reader. I know I can be quite a "matter of fact" kind of person and state things as I see them. A lot of it is in my nature, and I always say, "That's the way the cookie crumbles." I frequently stop and ponder, how in heaven's name did I get to where I am? It really has been a courageous journey for me when I think of my journey from that very, very small town in Brunei to my life now, doing things I never fathomed I would. I pinch myself constantly, and I still consider myself a small fish in a big pond in my field.

I am humbled by how things have panned out in my life but I do have to say that a lot of it is thanks to having courage, particularly the courage to fail. I have failed ceremoniously on many occasions though I can't remember most of them now. My attitude is to learn from the failure and improve from it. Move on! My school's motto was "Be strong and of good courage". These words still ring true in my heart.

Did you know the shell of a lobster is hard and inelastic and it must shed its shell in order to grow? Ecdysis, commonly called shedding, occurs when a lobster extrudes itself from its old shell. The overall process of preparing for, performing, and recovering from ecdysis is known as molting. Unlike animals that are soft-bodied and have skin, a lobster's shell, once hard, will not grow much more. Lobsters grow throughout their lives and therefore spend much of that time preparing for, or undergoing ecdysis.

There is so much we can learn from nature, right? The lobster leaving the shell temporarily makes it vulnerable but it must grow, like all of us. That's nature forcing it to grow. In our natural state, human beings don't have to but I do think we do, figuratively. We all have that nagging feeling when we're too comfortable, but are we taking heed of this? The natural inclination is the path of least resistance. And yes, we are going to feel a little vulnerable in the process of growing and changing.

I felt vulnerable leaving my cocoon in Brunei. I thought it was rather unfair I had to be kicked out of my comfort zone. I found it a big effort having to make new friends and proving myself academically. In the scheme of things, I am glad we spoke the same language so at least that wasn't so bad. I remember thinking, after graduation and settling into my first job, that I didn't want to get out of my comfort zone again ... or at least not for a very long time. Most of us get to a stage where we settle in a job or career so that we don't have to willingly grow again.

Now I want to talk about effort. I am glad I have arms and legs that work. There is work involved. Nothing falls from the sky. There are sacrifices. My twenties were spent working in the evenings (mostly during weekends) whilst having a day job. My friends had social lives and went out to parties but that took a back seat for me. Even holidays had to be well-crafted, well-timed and well-budgeted.

My thirties were spent building my network marketing business in the evenings and sometimes traipsing out of town working towards developing a passive income. I do have to say a foundation was set during those days, and I am still reaping the fruits of my labour to this day. No one sees the work you put in.

I cannot remember when I was doing just one thing or just one job. I treat these experiences as an investment in myself mentally and financially, knowing there will be a return on investment in due time. Plant corn, get corn. Plant time, get time. I am more wary of spending more time enjoying myself nowadays because like I said, we all want to follow the path of least resistance. However, I do get concerned if I am a little too relaxed.

Most people can picture a dog madly chasing a rabbit. For people who don't understand why you are working so hard, imagine the dog running around but they can't see the rabbit. It basically looks like a mad dog. That's what you look like to outsiders as you're spending the time building your dream and future. Only you can see the rabbit.

As cliché as it sounds, work works. If you're clear about what your dream is, even when it's a little fuzzy, work at it until it becomes clearer. The Eisenhower Decision Matrix helps people decide what to spend time on by seeing what's important and not urgent. I share this example of exercising every day. It's important and not urgent today, but in 10 years without exercise, it might become urgent and important when you are rushed to the hospital.

Don't let inertia set in. An idle mind (and hands) is the devil's workshop. Very soon, time will pass and you'll wonder how time has just flown. Success requires a spoonful of courage and bucketloads of effort. I have had experiences where my whole body has turned cold, my throat and lips are parched dry and I feel faint. From doing my first play to going on TV, courage takes courage. It can start with a spoonful but build it up from there.

Of Context and Intentions

I work in a talk radio station which covers largely business but also other subjects like politics, art and current affairs so I get my fair share of hearing bad news. It's one thing to know what's going on but another to be neutral about things. This can be challenging as we're not trained to be emotionally neutral or disconnected, plus sometimes, we have to be emotionally involved to cover a story well. I make it a point to disengage from certain stories and replace it with something positive. This is something I have to consciously do so I don't get worked up about things.

I purposely watch a lot of comedy or read other material which is uplifting. It is so important to keep my mind positive. We have a negative bias towards things, so that, even when things are of equal intensity, things of a more negative nature have a greater effect on our psychological state and processes than neutral or positive things. No wonder mental health is an even bigger issue now as we're bombarded by negative news 24 hours a day. Sometimes we feel helpless and hopeless.

From climate change, stinky politicians, racism, ageism, sizeism, cultural misappropriation, microaggressions to whatever is happening around the world, how do we keep our head above water and choose to see the positive and not the negative? It is conscious hard work to do so. Be conscious about what you're feeding yourself.

The reason I am bringing up this topic is also because we have become a sensitive lot of people. We flare up at everything and it's easy to comment and complain online hidden by a screen, acting as what we would call keyboard warriors or worse, cybertroopers. Most of the time, it's also not constructive criticisms where we offer suggestions but just comments like, "You're horrible" (that's the nicest kind of comment) without explaining why and how an individual can improve.

As an individual, how can we resolve this? There is a word in the Malay language called *niat*, or intention. We are not all natural communicators and sometimes the message would come out all wrong. For example, my mother and I would frequently be at loggerheads about something. I understand she is from a different generation. I would always question myself, "Is her intention good?" and if it is, I let it slide. I have even asked her at times, "What is your intention?" and if she doesn't have a good answer, I ignore it. I understand we're at that level of familiarity where I can question her.

But often, we're not. People will say things to you sometimes with the best intention but it'll come out wrongly. Take the high road and ignore it. Don't sweat the small stuff. Pray for discernment in your life with the people you meet. As we know, there are people who may say the nicest things but their intentions are not genuine. Again, be wary and choose wisely whether you want to participate or not. No point in winning the battle to lose the war.

Related to intentions is context. Let me give you an example here. Not too long ago, there was a white American girl who decided to wear a cheongsam for her high school prom. She posted this online and got a backlash from the Asian Americans. Although I am not Asian American and may not know the situation fully, I am sure the girl's intent was complimentary as she wore it to her prom, where people wear their best clothes, and not to Halloween as a costume or a joke!

There is also the story of the Masterchef Australia winner who took pride in her Chinese heritage when cooking but when greeted in Chinese (both Cantonese and Mandarin) by a white Australian over Australian radio said it was racist. Did you think his intent was to insult? A simple "I don't speak it" and maybe a personal message later would educate the individual better.

If there are things that need to be explained and there is an intention to educate, maybe speak one-on-one to the person and not abuse them for all and sundry to hear. Speak gently and provide reasons. We have seen the repercussions of bullying and cyberbullying. It doesn't help anyone!

The Japanese concept of *ikigai*, translated as "reason for being", teaches us that life is not about money and success, and that the accumulation of wealth is a by-product rather than the focus. Similarly, mastery in something is about growth, with mastery being a by-product. Meaning in life doesn't come from saving the world, but from connecting with family, friends, co-workers and the community. Beyond finding something you love and are passionate about, it's about living your values and finding meaning and purpose in daily living.

Every time I go for a walk, I take the time to appreciate nature, from the way the sun is shining to the direction the wind is blowing. Sometimes it's about counting the different types of hibiscus I can find on my walking path to how my body is feeling. Choose connection and harmony, rituals and small joys, creativity and flow and gratitude and contribution.

We can choose to be angry every day or we can take that energy and use it for something good. We have a choice every second, every minute and every day. We should choose to wake up every day and be grateful, find the joy in little things and be in the here and now.

Image credit: Zinq Studio

ACKNOWLEDGEMENTS

Behind every production, there is a team of people that supports it. Before I get into that, for all the effort I have put in, I know this is not possible without my Lord and Savior Jesus Christ, He who strengthens me in everything I do. I am humbled and always mindful that I am nothing without him.

I would like to thank Joanne Lim for designing the book cover. Joanne was a student of mine when I was a part-time lecturer in a college. As chance would have it, she recognised me at a restaurant and arranged lunch the following week. We caught up with our lives over the past decades and she delightfully offered to do my book cover. I am blessed.

I told Leon Tan the premise of my book was about life stages and to make the most of each life stage. Coming from the film industry, he came up with the current book title.

Writing the forward is one of my oldest and dearest friends George Aveling. He pored over my book and gave me such candid advice. I followed some of his advice and much to his chagrin, he still wrote the foreword for my book. Thank you dear George. I'll do better next time but I am too afraid to ask for your advice because I am not such a good student. Thank you however for always pushing me to be better and for asking the deep and meaningful questions that make me cringe in my seat.

I would like to dedicate this book to my father Bob, my mother Judy and my siblings Jeffry, Elberton and Sylvia, the ones I have known all my life and have supported me in my education. My mum has been my greatest cheerleader in everything I do. For that I am truly grateful. She never stopped in pursuing my dreams whatever they were and I had no gender stereotypes built into me growing up. I look back and am so glad that that was never in my consciousness.

My dearest son Jude Wong, who is currently at 17 almost 18 (at time of writing this), the age where they ignore their mother. Thank you for not being a handful and a joy to my life. You continue to be unimpressed with your mother but I know you love me. Thank you for your sense of humour. You keep me humbled and joy-filled.

Thank you to the wonderful team at Marshall Cavendish, especially Anita Teo, who doesn't know me from Adam but decided to give me a chance anyway. I am truly grateful. Thank you for this opportunity to work together and for trusting me on this pioneer project. I hope there will be more opportunities in the future.

ABOUT THE AUTHOR

Freda Liu is a vivacious persona who has lived and breathed business in the past decade with Malaysia's leading business radio station and has conducted over 5,000 interviews with prominent names like Stephen Covey, motivational speaker Nick Vujicic, former GE CEO Jack Welch, the Duke of York HRH Prince Andrew and Wikileaks founder Julian Assange. A broadcast and communication veteran, she is also a highly sought after moderator for corporate events, speaker for women empowerment and personal branding, trainer and coach.

She has authored five books: *PR Yourself*, *Shake & Spear Your Business: The Romeo & Juliet Way*, *Everybody Loves Ray*, *Bursting Fixed Mindsets* and *In Your Skin*.

Freda is a member of the National Association of Women Entrepreneurs Malaysia and the Malaysian Association of Professional Speakers. An advocate for improvement in sustainability and women empowerment, she is an ambassador for the Women of Global Change KL Chapter and a WASH (Clean Water & Sanitary Hygiene) advocate for World Vision Malaysia.

www.fredaliu.com